MW01009734

MY
SIMPLE
ITALIAN
**THEO
RANDALL**

To Holly

MY
SIMPLE
ITALIAN
THEO
RANDALL

100 inspired recipes from one of Britain's best Italian chefs

Best wishes

Theo Randall

EBURY
PRESS

For Chloe my god daughter

109876543

Ebury Press, an imprint of Ebury Publishing,
20 Vauxhall Bridge Road,
London, SW1V 2SA

Ebury Press is part of the Penguin Random House
group of companies whose addresses can be found
at global.penguinrandomhouse.com

Penguin
Random House
UK

Copyright © Theo Randall 2014
Photography © Martin Poole 2014

Theo Randall has asserted his right to be identified as
the author of this Work in accordance with the Copyright,
Designs and Patents Act 1988

First published by Ebury Press in 2015

www.penguin.co.uk

A CIP catalogue record for this book is available
from the British Library

Copyeditor: Norma Macmillan
Design: Smith & Gilmour
Photography: Martin Poole
Food stylist: Aya Nishimura
Stylist: Lydia Brun

ISBN: 9780091929015

Colour origination by Altaimage, London
Printed and bound in China by C&C Offset Printing Co., Ltd

Penguin Random House is committed to a sustainable future
for our business, our readers and our planet. This book is
made from Forest Stewardship Council® certified paper.

FSC
www.fsc.org
MIX
Paper from
responsible sources
FSC® C018179

Acknowledgements

Thanks to Alex and Emma Smith for telling me the anchovy joke
and making this book. Martin Poole for your brilliant photos and eating.
Aya Nishimura for the finishing touches that made all the difference. Lydia
Brun for choosing the best plates and creating the set. Sarah Lavelle
for getting the book started and listening to my ideas. Laura Higginson
for your patience and drive. Norma Macmillan for your attention to
detail and efficiency in the edit.

Thank you to Natalie, Max and Lola for your love.

Maria Wrazen for being such a lovely person. Thas Robinson for always
being there and sorting everything out. Theodore Hill for being such
a good friend and brilliant cook. Ivan Di Nasta for your professionalism
and pure love of what you give to people. Vanessa Mosca, thank you
for adding passion and consistency. Helen Douglas for your commitment
in driving everyone but being so humble in your achievements. Karen
Watt for your attention to detail and love of giving. Alvaro Rey for your
total support and passion. Luis Rodrigues for your commitment and
organisation. David Okogie for your loyalty and skill. Chris Beverly for
pure talent. Ben Richardson for always wanting to learn and having
the most amazing palate. Daniel Garland for being a brilliant cook.
Jonathan Lawson for your drive and passion (eye of the tiger).
Laurent Tse for being such a lovely person but also a really good
cook. David Meredith for laughing at my jokes and being my protégé.
Jonathan Rogers for being handsome, funny and a good cook.

My parents Peter and Rosemary Randall who installed a love of quality
of life from an early age. Ivor and Josselyn for always being there and
giving great advice. Marc and Sophie Cohen for loving my children
and teasing them (that's you Marc). Claudia and Chris Cain, for being
my sister and both of you always making me laugh. Justine Randall
and Paul Kelley for the lovely furniture, chocolate brownies – and
Justine your amazing tapestries. Max Tollemache and Beck for taking
Max and Lola out on a Friday night to the newest restaurants so I can
get the feed back. Limpet Baron and David Hughes for running the
finest tea room at the Chelsea Physic garden and also for being
such good friends. Auntie Fong and Nico for giving us our
beautiful golden labrador girls Evie and Maude.

Also to everyone who has worked and dined at my restaurant,
THANK YOU. x

contents

how long have you got?

introduction

I love cooking! It's such an enjoyable and fulfilling experience. I know you'll think that it's very easy for me to say this, but I truly believe that everyone should know how to cook – and, I hope, take pleasure from it.

Cooking is not all about presentation and technical methods. It's about making some delicious food and then sitting down and sharing it. There is nothing simpler than a boiled egg with some buttered toast, but if you have really good fresh eggs and lovely bread and butter then you have a feast. Good-quality ingredients have a great flavour already, so the cooking or preparation needed is minimal.

This book is all about simple recipes that do not require lengthy preparation. Some of the recipes have very few ingredients, but don't let that tempt you to add extra unnecessary ones. As the architect Mies van der Rohe said, 'Less is more'.

With simple dishes, the quality of the ingredients you use is very very important, and it helps if you have a storecupboard that is well stocked with jars and cans of things like olives, fish, capers and tomatoes, as well as packets of polenta, risotto rice, pasta and dried porcini. Combining these with fresh vegetables, meat, cheese and so on, you can put together a tasty dish with ease.

Be on the lookout for ingredients when you travel too. I always say that if you are in Italy and you see olive oil, dried porcini mushrooms, Parmesan cheese or balsamic vinegar, buy some because it will invariably be good quality and cheaper than at home – and it will add a bit more inspiration to your cooking. Nothing sounds better when you have friends over than telling them you got this amazing olive oil from a small market in southern Italy. Food always tastes better when it has a story.

Here's one of mine. A fish supplier phoned me up one afternoon when I was at The River Café. He was on the other line to one of his contacts on a dayboat that was fishing around Poole in Dorset. They had just caught a huge 10kg turbot and he thought we might buy it. Well we did. It just so happened that Steve Bird, the owner of the fish supplier Cove Shellfish, was coming into London that evening and promised me the huge turbot would be with us before service started. As always the traffic coming into Hammersmith was terrible so he was delayed, but during the waiters' briefing I told them we had this amazing fish on the menu that had been caught that afternoon. As the restaurant began to fill up, the orders started to come in on the main course for roasted turbot. Luckily Steve arrived just in time, and bold as he was walked through the restaurant holding this beautiful fish. I prepped it and we were cooking the turbot steaks within 10 minutes of it arriving. The fish sold out and everyone who had it still remembers eating it. That story is still being told.

choosing ingredients for the storecupboard

Good, flavoursome ingredients are key to the simple and straightforward recipes in this book, so here are a few tips on what to look for when you're shopping to stock your pantry.

Olive oil

Olive oil is THE essential ingredient, and I think you need two different olive oils in your storecupboard. The one to use for salads, bruschetta and soups should be a cold-pressed olive oil. All that means is that the crushed olives have not been heated during the pressing of the olive paste that produces the oil. An oil that is cold-pressed will be darker than a basic oil and the viscosity will be thicker. Make sure you keep this oil in a dark, cool place to ensure that it retains its green grassy flavour – olive oil is perishable so never keep it in the window or by the cooker.

For the second oil – to use for frying garlic for a tomato sauce, brushing over a whole fish to be roasted or making mayonnaise – buy an extra virgin olive oil that is not too light but has a fruity flavour. The lighter the oil, usually the more commercial it is – commercial oil is extracted from the olive paste but heated to high temperatures, so it tends to lack character and flavour. You can always tell these oils as they have a taste of cooked olives and tend to be a bit greasy.

If you cook a lot you might find it worthwhile to buy a 5-litre tin of olive oil from a supplier. A very good online supplier, with a fantastic selection of olive oils and vinegars. is www.theoliveoilco.com.

Balsamic vinegar

Most of the balsamic vinegars sold in shops and supermarkets are Balsamic Vinegar of Modena.

This is an inexpensive version of the real thing – Aceto Balsamico Tradizionale, which is produced from a reduction of cooked white Trebbiano grape juice and has been made since the Middle Ages in Modena and Reggio Emilia.

Aceto Balsamico Tradizionale has a very lengthy ageing process with storage in dramatic temperature changes, like a loft or an outhouse that gets the heat of the sun in the summer and very cold temperatures in the winter. The vinegars are kept in unusually shaped wooden barrels – they are long and shallow to create a larger surface area of vinegar to hasten evaporation (the barrel stoppers are left off with muslin in their place). This ageing process is what gives the vinegar its distinctive thick, sticky viscosity.

When you try the real balsamic vinegar you can instantly tell the difference between it and the inexpensive version because of the length of its flavour and its smoothness. You only need a few drops so a small bottle will last a very long time. It is traditionally served with fresh Parmesan cheese – a drop or two on top of a chunk. This is one of the best food combinations I know.

Tomatoes

Tomatoes are an extremely important ingredient in a lot of my recipes, both fresh and canned. There is nothing like making a tomato sauce with well-flavoured fresh tomatoes but unfortunately the season can be short. So I find making tomato sauce with canned tomatoes or jarred passata can be almost as good as long as you cook the sauce gently for at least 20 minutes, season well and add freshly torn basil.

When you are buying canned tomatoes always choose Italian. I find that chopped or crushed tomatoes in juice tend to make a richer, sweeter sauce than the standard whole peeled tomatoes, because those canned whole tend to be unripe – the main flavour comes from the tomato concentrate that has been added.

Cirio tomato passata has got a lovely consistency. Buy it in a screwtop jar, because if you don't need it all you can put the lid back on and keep it in the fridge.

Fish

A few recipes in the book use my favourite salted fish, anchovies – mainly as a seasoning, as in the dressing for Panzanella (see recipe on page 75). On their own anchovies are absolutely delicious but the quality has to be tip top. Canned anchovies packed in olive oil are my preference.

I think one of the best – and simplest – ways to eat anchovies is to place them in milk with some large sage leaves, then roll the wet anchovies in flour and press the sage leaves on top to create a sandwich; dip into a little batter and shallow fry in sunflower oil until the tiny parcels are golden and crisp. Serve with a squeeze of lemon.

Tuna fish, which is available packed in water, brine or oil, in both cans and jars, is more popular than ever. Like anchovies, the more expensive tends to be the best. I find the lighter the tuna, the better the flavour. Tuna packed in jars tends to be in olive oil, which is much heavier than tuna in brine, but whichever you use avoid chunked tuna as the amount you get from a can tends to be a lot more water than fish.

I think that all canned and jarred fish is very under-rated. I have early childhood memories of my mother's amazing dense bread, toasted and buttered, with a canned sardine (in olive oil) spread on top, seasoned with a squeeze of lemon and black pepper. It was heavenly!

Pulses

Chickpeas and beans such as borlotti and cannellini are a brilliant source of protein as well as being a very versatile ingredient. For speed and ease of preparation, there is nothing wrong with using those that are ready-cooked and they make a really useful storecupboard standby. I prefer chickpeas and beans packed in jars to those in cans, but both are good. The water in the jars can be slightly salty, so you might want to drain it off before using. Canned pulses can have a gloopy consistency, which is a bit unpleasant, so they benefit from a rinse before using.

A simple way to make a bit more of beans is to fry a little garlic in a saucepan, add some chopped parsley plus a dash of red wine vinegar and then tip in the contents of the jar or can. Finish with some olive oil and check the seasoning.

Unlike beans, ready-cooked lentils are canned in a delicious cooking liquid that is usually seasoned with bay leaves, carrot and celery. So you can just heat them up in the liquid. Using a can of lentils in a chicken liver and pancetta salad (see recipe on page 68) is fast food at its best.

Olives and capers

My favourite olives are the little black Ligurian Taggiasche and the large green Sicilian Noccelara del Bolice. If olives are packed in a brine, I find it's best to buy them in plastic tubs or jars that are sealed because the brine can go rancid if they are left exposed to the air for too long. When you see displays of olives in open bowls or trays in a shop, you will be able to tell if the brine is off – it will have a very earthy smell.

Capers are one of those ingredients that, a bit like anchovies, people love or hate. As you have probably guessed by the amount of recipes in this book that use them, I love capers. They come in all shapes and sizes, and probably the easiest to enjoy are the miniature ones packed in vinegar. For me, Sicilian capers are the finest, with the most flavour. They usually come in glass jars with shards of sea salt. You need to gently rinse off the salt before you use them. The most disappointing capers tend to be the very big ones that have been kept in a poor-quality vinegar. However, these can be very tasty if you drain off the vinegar and rinse the capers in cold water, then shallow-fry in hot olive oil – delicious with a lemon sole.

Marinated vegetables

I wouldn't recommend buying jars of vegetables marinated in seasoned olive oil as they tend to be tasteless, with just the flavour of the marinade they are in. There are exceptions of course but it's much better to prepare them yourself by simply grilling the vegetables on a ridged griddle pan or barbecue and then seasoning them with fresh basil and olive oil.

If you are feeling lazy you could use a jar of charred red peppers packed in oil and mix them with freshly grilled courgettes and aubergines. Just be sure to pop them in the oven or heat on a charcoal grill beforehand as they tend to lack the smokiness you get when you grill and peel peppers yourself.

Marinated artichokes in jars are actually quite good if you drain them from their brine and then season with salt and pepper, a squeeze of lemon, a teaspoon of chopped parsley and olive oil. This will give them a much more rounded flavour than the acid brine they were packed in. The best artichokes are, of course, those you prepare yourself (see below).

Chestnuts

Another useful ready-made product is vacuum-packed chestnuts. They are delicious in a soup or with some braised Savoy cabbage and pancetta (see the recipe for roast grey partridge on page 152). Nothing beats fresh chestnuts, of course, but it can be hard to get good ones and they require a fair amount of prep. (I find the easiest way is to score them, then boil for 10–15 minutes; when they're cool, cut them in half and either peel off the tough outer skins or just scoop out the flesh.) The vac-packed chestnuts are actually a purée that has been poured into chestnut-shaped moulds and pressed.

Speaking of chestnut purée, the canned sweetened purée from France is amazing – delicious with Crema di Mascarpone (see recipe on page 210) or on its own with grated dark chocolate.

Dried porcini

These have so many uses so are always good to have in your cupboard. But beware of the packets that have a little window showing beautiful big slices of mushroom, because these slices may well be covering up the small chopped bits that the packet is full of. Try to buy porcini in clear plastic wrapping so you can see what you are paying for. The rule of thumb is that the lighter in colour they are, the newer/fresher they are. When they become very dark, they can have an almost Marmite flavour, which can be overpowering. (To set the record straight, I love Marmite.)

Polenta and rice

Polenta comes in various forms (but never 'instant' in my kitchen). I think the best ones are bramata and bramata integrale, which is hearty and rustic in taste and texture because it's wholemeal. Bramata polenta is a bit more refined with a coarse, bright yellow grain that cooks beautifully. A good polenta will take at least half an hour to cook. Anything that cooks quicker than that will not have a good flavour or texture.

Risotto rice is easy to buy – you can find it in every supermarket now. I use Carnaroli because it is the most consistent in quality, and I think the most forgiving – it's harder to overcook than, say, Arborio. Look for Carnaroli in paper packets or cloth sacks rather than boxes.

Pasta

When it comes to buying pasta, expensive packaging usually means better quality, although there are exceptions. Other indications of good quality are a longer cooking time given on the packet, and if the packet states that it is 'bronze die'– this means the pasta will have a rougher, more sandpapery texture, ideal for the sauce to cling to so every piece of pasta tastes of the sauce. There is nothing wrong with cheaper varieties of pasta but they do tend to have a smooth surface that won't hold the sauce as well.

My favourite brands of dried egg pasta are Pasta di Aldo and Cipriani.

There are two golden rules for cooking pasta: 1) Make sure you cook all pasta 2–3 minutes less than the time the packet suggests, and 2) always remove the pasta from its cooking water – using tongs for long pasta and a slotted spoon for short pasta – and add it to the sauce with a ladle or two of the pasta water. DO NOT POUR THE PASTA INTO A COLANDER TO DRAIN AS THE STEAM WILL OVERCOOK THE PASTA AND IT WILL BECOME CONGEALED AND STUCK TOGETHER. Once the pasta is in the sauce, keep cooking until the pasta is chewy and the sauce has thickened from the pasta starch. Season and serve immediately – pasta waits for nobody!

You can buy lovely fresh pasta from delis and supermarkets, such as The Fresh Pasta Company's tagliarini, but the best I have found comes from specialist suppliers like Natoora. Or why not try making fresh pasta yourself, from tipo 00 flour, fine semolina flour and really good eggs (see recipe on page 89)? Practice makes perfect.

Pine nuts

I love pine nuts and have even been known to forage my own. But it's a lot easier to buy them! Look out for European pine nuts because they have much more flavour than the imported Asian variety. Those are smaller and stubby in shape, and tend to taste a bit rancid as they are never very well packaged.

Sea salt

When you go to a supermarket you see a lot of different sea salts, some very expensive. It's not always easy to make a choice. But I can emphatically say: DON'T BUY table salt. It has been chemically treated and has a very unpleasant flavour. My favourite sea salt is Maldon. It tastes really good and is widely available.

When you cook – whether it is blanching spinach or green beans or boiling potatoes or pasta – always add salt to the water. By doing so you are adding flavour to the ingredient but actually using little salt as the cooking water is where the majority of the salt remains. This way of seasoning is far healthier than adding salt at the table.

shopping for fresh foods

Supermarkets stock a fantastic selection of fresh foods and are always a good place to go to find jars, cans and dry goods. If you want something special, a trip to your local farmers' market is always a treat and a great opportunity to shop with your eyes. (I like to say, 'Shop with your eyes, not a list' – that way you never compromise on your produce. Shopping with a list is fine if you can find exactly everything on it, but that rarely happens.)

It's also very important to visit your local butcher and fishmonger as regularly as you can. These once-staples of our high street are now specialist shops and need to be supported as they offer so much to us. Meat and fish are not cheap, but try to buy a really good piece of fish or meat every now and then and enjoy it.

If you want really good cheese there are lots of online suppliers that will deliver to you (one of my favourites is www.natoora.co.uk). Or if you are lucky enough to have a cheese shop near you, buy from them as the cheese will be matured and kept well. This is so important with cheese as the flavour needs to develop – if a cheese is kept in a cold fridge this will never happen. It's a bit like hanging meat: if you don't hang it, it will be tough and tasteless.

Tomatoes

When you are buying fresh tomatoes, a simple rule is that the smaller they are, the higher their acidity – it is this, when they are ripe, that turns to sweetness. Big tomatoes like ox heart have lower acidity so they tend not to have as much flavour as the small ones, but they have great texture. Try mixing the two together – they will then taste even better as they complement each other's flavour.

I particularly like Datterini tomatoes, which are a small plum type that is very sweet and aromatic.

For a fresh tomato sauce always use ripe plum tomatoes. They are flavoursome and fleshy, which is what makes them ideal for sauce. When peeling them, don't just boil the kettle and pour the hot water on to them to blanch: they have a thick skin and benefit from being boiled for a couple of minutes. This will loosen the skin so they are easy to peel, and will also slightly break down the flesh, making the tomatoes taste better.

Globe artichokes

There are many ways to prepare artichokes, but this is the best if you have small, firm ones with long stems. First peel the stem, then use a sharp knife to cut around the base of the artichoke to remove the dark bitter leaves. Cut off the top and scoop out the choke in the middle. Finally, trim off any dark bits. As soon as you finish, put the artichoke into a bowl of water with some parsley stalks. The parsley will stop the artichoke discolouring. Most cookery books recommend lemon juice, but parsley is better as the lemon can overpower the flavour of the artichoke.

I was in Verona one November and in the beautiful Piazza delle Erbe I came upon a little old lady sitting at a tiny stall, surrounded by huge boxes of artichokes with their leaves and stems attached. She was preparing the hearts of this delicious vegetable by using a razor-sharp knife to cut the base and scoop out the choke with two quick movements. I was mesmerised by the speed with which she did this, and her ability to take the cash and bag up the artichokes all at the same time. I had to have a go so I asked if I could. She agreed and offered her stool as well. I declined the stool but did get an approving smile on my artichoke preparation.

Eggs

Always buy the freshest possible eggs. I think organic and small (or bantam) eggs have the best flavour, and my favourite brand is Clarence Court Burford Brown eggs. These have an amazing dark yellow yolk and are brilliant simply poached or boiled. Italian eggs are very good too and widely available. Hens in Italy are fed a diet of corn and carrots so the yolks are very dark yellow, almost orange – these are the eggs used to make the best pasta dough. If you use them in pastry and baking, you'll notice that your cakes and tart cases are a completely different colour.

One recipe that requires good fresh eggs is mayonnaise. People are often tempted to make huge quantities of mayonnaise, especially if using a food processor. The problem with this is you make too much for one meal, then put the rest in the fridge and by the next day it has probably split. So you throw it out, which is such a terrible waste of expensive ingredients. Make a small quantity and use it all.

Vegetables

I find that vegetables that grow in the ground always have more flavour if they still have a bit of earth on them. Compare a washed organic carrot, bought with soil on it and leaves attached, with a carrot from a plastic packet – eating them both raw with a home-made mayonnaise. The organic carrot will be sweet with a lovely aftertaste. The other carrot will also be sweet but will lack depth of flavour and will leave a rather unpleasant taste in your mouth. The same applies to potatoes. The best spuds to buy are the ones covered in mud.

We live in a world where most of our produce is washed and packaged for sale. That is never going to be good when it comes to flavour. My recommendation is if you can buy vegetables

(and fruit) loose – not worrying about them being uniform in shape and size – they will definitely taste better.

A good example of this is spinach. Most of the flavour in spinach is in the stems, which you won't get if you buy it in plastic packets. If you find it in bunches, keep the stems long for extra flavour. Also, blanch in boiling salted water, and do not refresh afterwards in cold water – this will just dilute the flavour of the spinach. Squeezing it hard to remove all the water until the spinach is dry is really removing all the goodness and flavour. Instead, simply pour the spinach and its cooking water into a large colander in the sink and leave it to cool down for 15 minutes, then use a metal or wooden spoon to press the spinach against the colander until all the excess water has gone.

I remember a meal many years ago at the winemakers Planeta in Sicily. We were having dinner with the Planeta family. A huge roasted grouper fish was presented at the table with their delicious pungent, grassy olive oil. Along with this was the best-tasting spinach I have ever eaten. Before dinner we had gone to meet the cooks in the kitchen and saw by the sink this huge colander full of blanched spinach. It was more like chard than spinach and had long stems attached. It was pressed in the colander by hand, then simply tossed in a bowl with a little sea salt and pepper before being served in colourful dishes.

On my plate I had an enormous piece of fish and I helped myself to an extra large portion of spinach on which I poured a generous amount of olive oil. The combination of the sweet-tasting roasted fish, the sweet earthy flavour of the spinach and the grassy olive oil was simply stunning. There was a huge plate of lemons on the table for squeezing on to the fish, but I decided against this as it was perfect as it was.

Cured meats (salumi)

Prosciutto di Parma, bresaola, fennel salami and so on can easily be found ready-sliced in the supermarket chiller cabinet. These are fine but they won't have the depth of flavour of salumi freshly sliced on a slicer at a good Italian deli. There is nothing like prosciutto di Parma that has been sliced in front of you to eat immediately.

On another trip to Verona I went to a brilliant restaurant just off the square of Piazza delle Erbe called Trattoria il Pompiere. As you walk in you are surrounded by photographs of the owner's family and famous dignitaries. Then you see the enormous display of prosciutto and salamis in every shape and size. And Lardo di Colonnata, bresaola, mortadella… These are perfectly sliced on to large white china plates and served with delicious pickles and fresh focaccia. When salumi are sliced with this care and attention, they taste fantastic. (The risotto at il Pompiere is one of the best in Verona.)

Cheese

Good buffalo mozzarella is hard to beat. Over the years this cheese has become almost a staple in delis and supermarkets, but there is a huge difference between the mozzarella you buy from the farm in and around Naples and the supermarket mozzarella in tubs. In Naples, the locals will buy mozzarella and almost eat it on the way home because it is considered at its best as soon as it is made. The texture is chewy and you really taste the creaminess of the water buffalo's milk. The mozzarella you get here is still delicious but doesn't have the same texture.

For me a Caprese is still the best way to eat buffalo mozzarella. Make sure your tomatoes are ripe and at room temperature, otherwise the simplicity of the tomato, fresh basil and mozzarella salad is ruined.

Parmigiano Reggiano is the king of Italian cheese and its method of production has never changed since it was first made many centuries ago. It is really not surprising that Parmesan cheese, as we call it, costs so much. It takes 500 litres of semi-skimmed milk to produce one 35–40kg cheese, and it needs at least 18 months to mature, with constant attention. We tend to serve Parmesan cheese with pasta, but in Italy they like to eat it on its own in chunks with a little drizzle of proper aged balsamic vinegar.

I remember a trip to Emilia Romagna and having lunch in a restaurant, which started with a chilled glass of deep purple Lambrusco that was so delicious. It was served with pane fritto (deep-fried short pastry), plates of prosciutto di Parma, chunks of Parmesan and a really old balsamic vinegar. I picked up the pane fritto, made a hole in the middle and placed a slice of prosciutto in it, then added Parmesan and a drop or two of balsamic vinegar. Wow, what a combination! It was all the best bits of Emilia Romagna in one mouthful.

It's hard to find really good ricotta – the type you see in a supermarket is typically the whipped version that has had double cream added to lengthen its shelf life. If you go to a specialist cheese shop or an Italian deli you will find a better product. Good ricotta should be firm enough so you can slice it.

I hope you enjoy cooking with this book as much as I have enjoyed writing it. As every chef writes in his or her book – HAPPY COOKING!

small plates
for starters, snacks and canapés

The recipes in this first chapter are easy and uncomplicated. I've designed them to be prepared ahead or made quickly and put on the table to share or to serve as a starter, so that when you're having people over you can enjoy their company rather than getting stressed in the kitchen. Some are dishes you can put together without too much fuss when a friend comes over unannounced, while others can be turned into canapés for a pre-dinner nibble with an Aperol Spritz. Two or three of these dishes could even make a great light lunch with some good fresh bread, olive oil and balsamic vinegar.

1 loaf of ciabatta bread
400g Datterini or cherry tomatoes,
    preferably mixed colours
8 basil leaves, chopped, plus
    extra chopped basil to finish
6 tbsp extra virgin olive oil, plus
    extra for drizzling
1 garlic clove, peeled
250g fresh ricotta
sea salt and freshly ground
    black pepper

Try to get good-quality ricotta for this as it makes all the difference. I remember when I went to Sicily with my friend Ossie Gray and we visited an olive oil producer. She was taking us out for dinner but said we had to stop off at a friend's house first because he had just got some fresh ricotta from a shepherd friend of hers. We went into his house and there in the middle of the kitchen table was a warm, perfectly moulded, fresh ricotta. I was offered a slice with some new oil poured on top. I ate it in seconds and asked for more. I think I ate half of that ricotta! Ever since I only cook with or eat 'proper' ricotta. Most of the commercial ricotta has cream added to it to give it a longer shelf life. It's nowhere near the same as the real thing. Serves 12 as a canapé with drinks.

crostini
with crushed tomatoes, basil and fresh ricotta

1 Preheat the oven to 180°C. Cut the ciabatta into 2cm slices. Lay them on a baking sheet and toast in the oven until they are lightly golden on each side. Remove from the oven and leave to cool.

2 While the ciabatta is toasting, chop the tomatoes into small pieces. Put them in a bowl with the chopped basil, olive oil and seasoning. Crush them with a spoon so the juices come out and you get a lovely wet tomato sludge.

3 Rub the garlic clove over one side of each slice of toasted ciabatta bread, then top with a spoonful of the tomatoes. Spread them over the toasted bread, pushing them in. Add a few spoons of ricotta on top and a good drizzle of olive oil, then finish with some extra chopped basil and a grinding of pepper.

200g ripe plum tomatoes
4 basil leaves, chopped
3 tbsp extra virgin olive oil,
    plus extra to finish
1 garlic clove, peeled
4 generous slices of sourdough
    bread, toasted
100g fresh goats' curd
8 black olives, preferably Taggiasche,
    pitted and finely chopped
sea salt and freshly ground
    black pepper

This is a perfect snack to make when you have people over. It can easily be a starter if you serve a couple each. Goats' curd is very fresh goats' cheese that hasn't been left to mature at all and form a rind, so it's really creamy. The bruschetta is great with an Aperol Spritz. Serves 4 as a snack or 2 as a starter.

bruschetta
with plum tomatoes, olives and fresh goats' curd

1 Chop the tomatoes into small pieces. Sprinkle with a good pinch of sea salt, then put the tomatoes in a sieve and leave to drain for a few minutes (the salt will draw out the excess liquid and concentrate the tomato flavour).

2 Mix the basil into the drained tomatoes, then tip into a bowl and stir in the olive oil. Use a wooden spoon to mash up the tomatoes a bit. Check the seasoning.

3 Rub the garlic clove over one side of each slice of toasted bread, then add a good spoonful of tomatoes and push down firmly so the tomatoes get absorbed into the bread.

4 Break up the goats' curd and place little bits on top of the tomatoes, then add the chopped olives. Finish with a drizzle of olive oil.

For the sauce
8 garlic cloves, peeled
150ml extra virgin olive oil
12 anchovy fillets (packed in oil), drained
1 tbsp good-quality red wine vinegar

For the vegetables
4 globe artichokes with long stems
4 young carrots, peeled
4 jerusalem artichokes, peeled and halved
1 head of romanesco, separated into florets
2 red peppers
1 large leaf of Swiss chard, quartered

bagna cauda

This is a traditional sauce of Piedmont, which may seem strange as Piedmont is not close to the sea for the anchovies. The reason, so the story goes, is that many years ago the Venetians would trade salted fish like anchovies for the Barolo wines and would cure the little fish in the wine barrels. This version of Bagna Cauda has no butter or cream, just olive oil. If you want a very smooth sauce you can add a spoon of cream. Traditionally an egg or two was added to the saucepan the Bagna Cauda was cooked in – waste not, want not! Serves 4.

1 Start with the sauce. If any of the garlic cloves have a central green 'germ', remove it. Put the garlic cloves in a small pan with the olive oil and cook on a very low heat for about 30 minutes until very soft but without any colour.

2 Meanwhile, prepare the vegetables. Peel the globe artichoke stems to remove all the tough fibrous outside, then cook the artichokes whole in boiling salted water for about 15 minutes until tender: you should be able to put a knife through the stem and the heart of the artichoke with ease. Drain. Peel off the outer leaves, then cut each artichoke lengthways in half and scoop out the choke.

recipe continues overleaf

bagna cauda *continued*

3 Bring another saucepan of salted water to the boil. Add the carrots, jerusalem artichokes and romanesco and simmer for about 5 minutes until they are almost cooked. Drain and set aside.

4 Preheat the grill, then char the red peppers all over. Place them in a bowl and cover with clingfilm. Leave to cool for 10 minutes before scraping off the charred skin with a serrated knife. Cut the peppers into wide strips, discard the seeds, then set aside.

5 Remove the garlic pan from the heat. Pour off the oil and keep to one side. Add the anchovies to the garlic cloves and mash to a paste. Add the vinegar with the reserved olive oil and mix with the paste.

6 Set the pan of anchovy sauce on a low heat and leave to warm through while you blanch the Swiss chard in boiling salted water, and heat the carrots, jerusalem artichokes, romanesco and globe artichokes in a separate pan of boiling salted water. After a minute, drain all the vegetables and dry on a cloth. Arrange all the vegetables (including the red peppers) on a plate, pour over the warm sauce and serve.

8 slices of ciabatta, 2cm thick
extra virgin olive oil
250g fresh chicken livers
50g unsalted butter
50g prosciutto di Parma, finely chopped
3 sage leaves, finely chopped
50ml sweet Marsala wine
sea salt and freshly ground black pepper

Chicken livers are cheap and delicious, and easily available from supermarkets. They're perfect in this snack, which is a typical *stuzzichini*, or sharing appetiser, in Italian trattorias. It's a great intro to a meal with a good glass of Chianti. Serves 8 as a snack or starter.

hot chicken livers
on crostini

1 Preheat the oven to 180°C. Spread the ciabatta slices on a baking sheet and drizzle over some olive oil. Bake for about 5 minutes until crisp and lightly golden. Remove from the oven and keep warm.

2 While the ciabatta is baking, trim off any greenish bits and visible sinew from the chicken livers.

3 Melt the butter in a hot frying pan, add the prosciutto and sage and cook for 1 minute. Season the chicken livers, then add them to the pan. Cook for 2 minutes on each side so they take on a nice golden colour.

4 Add the Marsala and remove from the heat. Leave the livers to carry on cooking in the residual heat of the pan for about 2 minutes.

5 When the livers have cooled down a bit but are still warm, spoon them on to the toasted ciabatta, spreading and pressing the livers so they break up and their juices are soaked up by the bread. Serve warm.

juice of 2 lemons
4 large globe artichokes with long stems
3 tbsp extra virgin olive oil
1 garlic clove, sliced
150ml dry white wine
2 tbsp roughly chopped flat-leaf parsley
sea salt and freshly ground black pepper
lemon halves, to serve

If you go to Rome between November and March you'll see this beautiful dish on most menus. The artichokes traditionally used are big and thus older and tougher, which is why they are normally braised – once trimmed they're cooked slowly with garlic, white wine, olive oil and parsley. If you love artichokes like I do, you'll agree that this is one of the best ways to eat them. Serves 4.

carciofi alla romana

1 First fill a large bowl with water and add the lemon juice (or a handful of parsley stalks, which will do the same job), then prepare the artichokes one at a time. Remove the tough outer leaves, then cut 2cm off the top, which should expose the furry choke. With a teaspoon, scoop out the choke – this should come out easily if the artichokes are fresh.

2 Trim the stem to about 10cm in length (assuming you are using long-stem artichokes), then use a potato peeler to remove the tough, stringy outer part of the stem. To ensure you remove enough, before you start peeling check the end of the stem to see how big the tender core is, then peel until all you can see is the core, with no other stem around it.

3 Next, turn the artichoke upside down so the stem is pointing upwards, and peel off any dark green bits from around the base and sides of the artichoke. Without delay, immerse the artichoke in the lemon water solution to prevent it from turning brown.

4 Heat the olive oil in a deep, heavy-based saucepan. Place the artichokes, face down, in the pan and add the garlic. Fry for about 2 minutes, then add the white wine, 200ml water and a pinch of salt. Put on a tight-fitting lid and cook on a very low heat for about 15 minutes. Turn the artichokes on their sides and cook for a further 5 minutes to cook the stems. Remove the lid and boil to reduce the cooking juices if necessary.

5 Add the chopped parsley and cook for another 5 minutes. The artichokes should be tender at this stage (the best way to check is to put a sharp knife through the middle of the choke – if the knife doesn't slip through very easily then add a little more water to the pan and continue cooking until the artichokes are tender).

6 Sprinkle with the remaining lemon juice and black pepper, then serve with the cooking juices and lemon halves.

240g ricotta
2 tbsp chopped basil
2 litres sunflower oil, for deep-frying
12 small courgettes with their flowers attached
sea salt and freshly ground black pepper
lemon, to serve

For the batter
300g tipo 00 flour
4 tbsp extra virgin olive oil
250ml warm water
1 organic egg white

It's not easy to buy courgette flowers, but they are becoming more widely available. If you are growing your own courgettes, you'll want to try this dish. The addition of ricotta and herbs just makes the flowers a bit more substantial. Serves 4.

deep-fried courgette flowers
stuffed with ricotta and herbs

1 First make the batter. Put the flour into a large mixing bowl and make a well in the middle. Pour the olive oil into the well, then mix the oil and flour together while slowly adding the warm water. Mix until the batter is smooth with the consistency of double cream. Set aside.

2 Combine the ricotta and basil and season with salt and pepper. Spoon into a piping bag fitted with a plain nozzle.

3 Put a deep pan containing the sunflower oil on to heat to 180°C. Preheat a warm oven.

4 Meanwhile, fill the courgette flowers: make a small hole in the side of each flower and gently pipe in some ricotta mix. Don't overfill the flower or it will burst during frying.

5 When the oil is nearly up to temperature, in another bowl whisk the egg white to soft peaks, then carefully fold into the batter.

6 Fry the flowers a few at a time so the pan isn't crowded: dip them (and their courgettes) into the batter and knock off any excess batter, then add to the hot oil. Deep-fry for about 3 minutes until crisp and light brown all over. Drain on kitchen paper and keep hot in the oven while cooking the rest of the batches. Serve hot with lemon wedges and sea salt.

juice of 1 lemon
3 violet artichokes with long stems
2 portobello mushrooms, cut into 1cm slices
6 small courgettes with their flowers attached
2 litres sunflower oil, for deep-frying
6 large sage leaves
4 small Swiss chard leaves
sea salt and freshly ground black pepper
lemon wedges, to serve

For the batter
300g tipo 00 flour
4 tbsp extra virgin olive oil
250ml warm water
1 organic egg white

Fresh green vegetables like artichokes, courgettes and Swiss chard are delicious coated in a light batter and gently deep-fried with some pungent sage leaves, then served with fresh lemon and sea salt. I've added portobello mushroom as it is so good deep-fried – it seems to concentrate the natural flavour. Serves 4.

fritto misto di vedura

1 First fill a large bowl with water and add the lemon juice (or a handful of parsley stalks, which will do the same job), then prepare the artichokes one at a time. Remove the tough outer leaves to reveal the pale inner heart. Open the heart and, using a teaspoon, scoop out the hairy choke. Peel the stem to remove the tough outside, leaving just the tender core. Chop the artichoke vertically in half, then cut into slices. Without delay, immerse the artichoke in the lemon water solution to prevent it from turning brown.

2 Next make the batter. Put the flour into a large mixing bowl and make a well in the middle. Pour the olive oil into the well, then mix the oil and flour together while slowly adding the warm water. Mix until the batter is smooth with the consistency of double cream.

3 Put a deep, heavy-based pan containing the sunflower oil on to heat to 180°C. Preheat a warm oven.

4 Drain the artichokes and dry on kitchen paper.

5 When the oil is nearly up to temperature, in another bowl whisk the egg white to soft peaks, then carefully fold into the batter.

6 Fry the vegetables in batches, each type separately (sage leaves with the chard): dip the vegetables into the batter and shake off excess, then deep-fry in the hot oil for 3–4 minutes until crisp and golden brown all over. Drain on kitchen paper and keep hot in the oven while you batter and deep-fry the remaining batches.

7 Season the fritto misto with salt and pepper and serve with lemon wedges.

300g fresh porcini mushrooms
2 tbsp extra virgin olive oil
1 garlic clove, thinly sliced
1 tsp chopped thyme
sea salt and freshly ground black pepper
sourdough or crusty bread, to serve

I love cooking porcini this way because you get such lovely flavoursome juices. Fresh porcini are unbeatable but you could also do this with portobello mushrooms. Serve with some really decent bread. Serves 2.

porcini in a bag

1 Preheat the oven to 180°C. Trim the mushroom stems and, using a tea towel, wipe the caps to remove any sand or dirt. Cut the porcini into 5mm slices.

2 Take two large sheets of greaseproof paper. Fold each in half, then open them up again. For each parcel, drizzle olive oil on to the centre of one half of each sheet of paper and top with half the porcini, garlic, thyme and plenty of seasoning. Fold over the other half of the paper to enclose the porcini and scrunch the edges together to make a half-moon-shaped parcel that is totally sealed.

3 Set the bags on a baking sheet and place in the oven. Bake for 15 minutes. Serve in the paper, with some sourdough or crusty olive-oil-based bread so you can mop up all the juices.

250g Bramata polenta flour
75g unsalted butter
fresh white truffle, to finish (optional)

For the fonduta
100g strong fontina cheese,
    cut into cubes
100ml full-fat milk
75g Parmesan cheese,
    freshly grated
2 organic egg yolks
sea salt and freshly ground
    black pepper

Polenta is not everyone's favourite dish, but if you make it with good-quality Bramata flour it is truly delicious. The inspiration for this recipe came from a visit to the town of La Morra in Piedmont, in the heart of the wine region. We had an exceptional dinner in a restaurant called Belvedere. The dish that stood out was a deep bowl containing a layer of wet polenta topped with a layer of melted fontina cheese and then an egg yolk, then more cheese and more polenta on top. This was duly covered with a very generous amount of shaved white truffle. It was amazing! Polenta does have a season – be sure to check the packing date on the box as polenta loses its flavour when it gets old. Serves 4.

wet polenta
with fonduta and white truffles

1 For the fonduta, soak the fontina cheese in the milk for 30 minutes.

2 Meanwhile, bring 1 litre water to the boil in a saucepan. Add a generous pinch of salt, then slowly pour in the polenta while whisking so it doesn't form lumps. Simmer over a low heat for 30 minutes, stirring occasionally.

3 Remove the cheese from the milk and set aside. Pour the milk into a heavy-based saucepan and bring to the boil. Remove from the heat and use a wooden spoon

to beat the fontina and Parmesan into the hot milk. The mixture should become thick and creamy. Add the egg yolks and season with salt and pepper. Set aside.

4 When the polenta is cooked (the best way to tell is if the polenta comes away from the sides of the pan), mix in the butter and season with salt and pepper.

5 Pour the polenta into a bowl and spoon over the fonduta. If you can get hold of a fresh white truffle, shave some on top. Serve hot.

1 x 250g piece beef fillet (centre-cut)
extra virgin olive oil
1 tsp chopped thyme
300g small beetroots,
    with their leaves if available
lemon juice
sea salt and freshly ground
    black pepper

For the horseradish sauce
150g fresh horseradish root
150ml crème fraîche
1 tsp red wine vinegar

Fillet is lean and tender, but not the tastiest cut of beef to cook. However, if you have it raw prepared like this it is really delicious. Ask your butcher for a piece of fillet from a beef sirloin that has been properly hung. That way you will get a lovely piece of meat that is not wet from being packed in plastic. When beef is hung for three to four weeks it can lose up to 30 per cent of its slaughter weight, which develops and concentrates the flavour. When fresh horseradish isn't in season, you can make the sauce using bottled grated horseradish (not creamed horseradish). Serves 4.

beef carpaccio
with beetroot and horseradish

1 Rub the beef fillet all over with about 1 teaspoon olive oil and sprinkle over the thyme. Heat a ridged grill pan until very hot, then sear the fillet for 30 seconds on each side. Remove from the pan and set aside to cool.

2 Meanwhile, cook the beetroots in boiling water until you can put a knife through – about 20 minutes for small beetroots and 30 minutes for larger ones. Drain and set aside to cool. In another pan, blanch the beetroot leaves for 5 minutes until tender; drain and refresh in cold water.

3 While the beetroots are cooking, make the sauce. Peel and grate the horseradish, then mix with the crème fraîche and vinegar. Season. Set aside.

4 Slice the fillet thinly. Lay the slices carefully, in one layer, between two sheets of greaseproof paper. Roll over them using a rolling pin to flatten and make them as thin as possible without breaking the meat.

5 Divide the fillet slices among four plates, or place the slices on a platter, laying them flat. Season with lemon juice, olive oil, salt and pepper.

6 Peel the beetroots, then slice them thinly. Toss the blanched leaves with olive oil, lemon juice and seasoning. Scatter the beetroot slices and leaves over the beef carpaccio and serve with the horseradish sauce.

1 medium courgette
1 lemon, cut in half
2 tbsp extra virgin olive oil
150g thinly sliced bresaola
50g wild rocket
100g Parmesan cheese (in a piece)
sea salt and freshly ground black pepper

Freshly shaved courgettes add good colour to this dish and is actually one of the nicest ways to eat them. Try to avoid using a big marrow-like courgette – a firm medium-sized one is best – and cut it on a mandoline before dressing with olive oil and lemon. Serves 2.

bresaola
with shaved courgette, rocket and parmesan

1 Cut the ends off the courgette, then slice it very thinly on a mandoline. Put the slices in a bowl. Squeeze the juice from half the lemon over them and add 1 tablespoon olive oil. Season with salt and pepper and toss together. Leave to one side to marinate for a few minutes.

2 Meanwhile, arrange the bresaola on two large plates so the slices are just overlapping. Squeeze the remaining lemon half over the bresaola and drizzle over the remaining olive oil. Scatter the rocket on the bresaola and add the marinated courgette slices.

3 Using a sharp paring knife, cut thin slivers of Parmesan and scatter them on top.

1 small head of radicchio,
   leaves separated
½ lemon
1 tsp aged balsamic vinegar
3 tbsp extra virgin olive oil
8 slices prosciutto di Parma
piece of Parmesan cheese
1 tsp chopped marjoram
sea salt and freshly ground
   black pepper

This is a perfect sharing antipasti dish. I love it because of the bright colour of the radicchio. This vegetable can be rather bitter, but blanching makes it lovely and sweet. You need a really good balsamic vinegar to dress it. When you cut the Parmesan, aim for slightly rough pieces. You tend to lose the true flavour of Parmesan if it is cut too thin. Serves 2.

prosciutto di parma
with marinated radicchio

1 Blanch the radicchio leaves in a pan of boiling salted water for 2 minutes until tender. Drain in a colander and cool down. When the radicchio is warm but not hot, gently squeeze it so it is not too wet.

2 Place the radicchio in a bowl and squeeze the lemon juice on top. Add the balsamic vinegar and salt and pepper to taste. Toss together. The radicchio will go an amazing bright red colour at this point. Add the olive oil and toss again, then check the seasoning is right.

3 Arrange the prosciutto slices on a large flat plate and scatter the radicchio on top. Using a small sharp knife, cut some pieces of Parmesan – as much as you like – and scatter them on the radicchio, along with the marjoram. Serve with bread.

1 x 500g piece of beef fillet (tail)
4 tbsp extra virgin olive oil
1 tsp chopped thyme
150g Datterini or cherry tomatoes,
   cut into quarters
100g wild rocket
juice of ½ lemon
1 tsp aged balsamic vinegar
75g Parmesan cheese shavings
sea salt and freshly ground black pepper

This is a great way to serve a seared piece of fillet. The crusting of the thyme and sea salt on the outside gives it a lovely flavour and texture. Being such a simple dish, it is all about good ingredients – the tomatoes should be sweet and the Parmesan fresh. If you have some good balsamic vinegar, use it on this because it will work really well with the other ingredients. Serves 4.

tagliata di manzo

1 Rub the fillet with 1 tablespoon olive oil, then sprinkle over the thyme and season with salt and pepper.

2 Heat a heavy-based frying pan. Add the fillet and cook for 3–4 minutes, turning frequently to ensure an even searing that gives the meat a browned crust. Remove from the pan and leave to rest for 3 minutes.

3 Meanwhile, combine the tomatoes and rocket in a large bowl. Add the remaining olive oil and the lemon juice. Season to taste. Toss gently together, then spread the rocket and tomatoes on a large plate.

4 Thinly slice the beef and arrange on top of the rocket and tomatoes. Drizzle the balsamic vinegar over the beef and add a grinding of black pepper. Finish with the Parmesan shavings.

3 tbsp extra virgin olive oil
2 garlic cloves, sliced
1 x 400g can chopped tomatoes
   or tomato passata
small bunch of basil
1kg fresh clams in shell (palourde)
2 fresh red chillies, chopped
sea salt and freshly ground black pepper

'Vongole' is usually associated with spaghetti but this is another very good way of enjoying sweet clams, with a rich tomato broth. When well-flavoured tomatoes are in season, use them. Select very ripe tomatoes, and peel and finely chop them. Serve the clams with extra virgin olive oil and Italian bread to dip in the sauce. Serves 2.

vongole veraci
with tomato sauce

1 Heat 2 teaspoons of the olive oil in a large heavy-based saucepan. Add half the garlic and cook briefly until it turns a light golden brown.

2 Add the canned tomatoes or passata with some of the basil leaves and stir, then cook over a medium heat for 20 minutes (or 10 minutes if using passata) until thick, stirring occasionally.

3 Meanwhile, put the clams in a colander and rinse thoroughly under cold running water, shaking the colander vigorously. Discard any clams that remain open.

4 Towards the end of the simmering time for the tomato sauce, heat the remaining olive oil in a shallow pan with the rest of the garlic and the chillies. Add the clams and stir. Cover and steam for 2–3 minutes until the shells are open. Discard any that remain closed.

5 Add the tomato sauce and stir through. Season with salt and pepper and add the rest of the basil leaves, roughly torn. Serve hot.

1 very fresh sea bass fillet, about 200g
1 tsp chopped marjoram
1 tsp chopped fresh red chilli
2 tbsp extra virgin olive oil
4 Datterini or cherry tomatoes,
   cut into quarters
wild rocket
sea salt and freshly ground
   black pepper

I like to use small wild sea bass for this carpaccio because they are so tender. You don't need any lemon – the tomatoes have enough acidity and adding lemon would make the dish too acidic. Serves 2.

sea bass carpaccio

1 Using a very sharp knife, slice the sea bass fillet downwards towards the skin into slices as thin as possible; discard the skin. Lay the slices on two plates or a platter.

2 Season with salt and pepper, then sprinkle with the marjoram and chilli. Drizzle over the olive oil and scatter the tomatoes on top. Finish with some rocket leaves.

soups, salads and egg dishes
for lunches and suppers

My recipes here for soups, salads and egg dishes are a versatile bunch – some are just right as a starter before a main course, while others are perfect for lunch, brunch at the weekend or a simple midweek supper. Almost all will take less than 30 minutes of hands-on time to prepare. I know I've said it before, but it's worth mentioning again: with top quality ingredients to get maximum flavour and texture, even the simplest of dishes can be sublime. I remember being on a school skiing trip and having to get up very early in the morning to get the first ski lift near to the top of Mont Blanc. One day we skied halfway down to a restaurant for breakfast/brunch. We were all really hungry. After the most amazing hot chocolate we were served huge plates with a perfectly crisp rösti potato, fried eggs and crispy rashers of smoked bacon. It was so wonderful, so simple, that I've never forgotten it and it has inspired many versions. In this chapter is my latest one – rösti potatoes with poached eggs and pizzaiola sauce.

1kg courgettes
1 tbsp extra virgin olive oil
1 garlic clove, finely chopped
10 basil leaves, chopped
8 courgette flowers
1 litre fresh chicken stock
200ml double cream
sea salt and freshly ground black pepper
freshly grated Parmesan cheese, to serve

This recipe requires the freshest courgettes, so if you are growing them this is the perfect dish to try. The flavour of the soup will develop once it is chilled. Serves 4 as a starter.

chilled courgette soup

1 Cut the courgettes into 5mm slices using a mandoline or sharp knife. Heat the olive oil in a saucepan and fry the courgettes with the garlic and half the basil on a low heat, stirring occasionally, for 5–8 minutes until the courgettes start to go a light golden colour.

2 Add the torn courgette flowers and pour in the chicken stock. Bring to the boil, then reduce the heat and simmer for 5 minutes.

3 Stir in the double cream. Add the remaining basil with salt and pepper to taste.

4 Pour the soup into a bowl and set in another bowl of iced water to cool (serve the soup as chilled as you like). Serve with grated Parmesan to sprinkle over.

2 tbsp extra virgin olive oil
3 celery sticks, finely chopped
1 red onion, chopped
2 carrots, chopped
1 garlic clove, finely sliced
2 x 400g cans chopped tomatoes
1kg Swiss chard
1 x 400g jar or can borlotti beans,
   drained (rinse if canned)
5 basil leaves
sea salt and freshly ground
   black pepper
fruity olive oil, to serve

A delicious soup, this is a meal in itself and is also very healthy. It's perfect for a cold day when not much is fresh in season. Serves 6 as a starter.

minestrone verde

1 Heat the olive oil in a large saucepan. Add the celery, onion, carrots and garlic and cook on a low heat for 20 minutes until soft, stirring occasionally.

2 Tip in the tomatoes and stir, then cook for a further 20 minutes, stirring from time to time.

3 Meanwhile, remove the Swiss chard leaves from the stalks. Finely chop the stalks; keep the leaves whole. Blanch the leaves in a large pan of boiling salted water for about 3 minutes until tender. Remove with tongs to a colander to drain, then roughly chop and set aside.

4 Add the chopped stalks to the pan of boiling water and cook for 3 minutes until tender; drain well in the colander set over a bowl (reserve the blanching water). Set the stalks aside.

5 Add the borlotti beans to the tomato mixture and cook for a further 10 minutes before pouring in 400ml of the chard blanching water. Bring to the boil, then simmer for 5 minutes.

6 Add the chard leaves and stalks along with the basil. Season with salt and pepper. If you want a smoother soup, blitz it for 10 seconds using a hand blender – this will give you a creamy but still chunky consistency. Serve the soup hot, with a good dash of fruity olive oil added to each bowl.

4 Charlotte potatoes, peeled
   and cut into 1cm pieces
1 tbsp extra virgin olive oil
2 tbsp finely chopped carrot
2 tbsp finely chopped onion
2 tbsp finely chopped celery
1 tsp chopped thyme
2 heaped tbsp pancetta cubes
1 garlic clove, finely sliced
12 freshly shucked oysters
   (with their liquor), chopped
100ml milk
5 tbsp double cream
1 tbsp chopped flat-leaf parsley
sea salt and freshly ground
   black pepper

Oysters are mostly served raw but this is a great way to cook them. You still get that oyster taste, but with the addition of pancetta, cream and potatoes to make a rich and satisfying soup. When you buy your oysters from a fishmonger, or the fresh fish counter in a supermarket, you can ask for them to be opened, or 'shucked'. Be sure you get all the liquor from their shells too. Serves 4 as a starter.

oyster soup

1 Parboil the potatoes in a pan of boiling salted water for 5 minutes until tender. Drain and set aside.

2 Heat the olive oil in a saucepan. Add the carrot, onion, celery, thyme, pancetta and garlic and cook for 5 minutes until the vegetables are soft.

3 Add the oyster liquor, milk, cream and potatoes. Bring to a simmer, then add the chopped oysters and parsley. Simmer gently for 3 minutes.

4 Season with salt and pepper to taste before serving.

150g asparagus, chopped
100g shelled fresh peas
100g shelled fresh, small broad beans
150g fine French beans, chopped
extra virgin olive oil
2 spring onions, finely chopped
¼ head of celery, finely chopped
200g waxy potatoes, peeled and cut into 1cm
   cubes
500ml fresh chicken stock (for home-made, see
   recipe on page 219)
50ml double cream
sea salt and freshly ground black pepper
Pesto (see page 220), to serve

'Primavera' indicates the start of the new season, and this is the first soup we make in the restaurant when peas, broad beans and asparagus appear. The trick is to have a smooth base and chunky pieces of the vegetables. The soup can be served either hot or cold. Serves 4 as a substantial starter or for lunch.

minestrone primavera

1 Blanch the asparagus, peas, broad beans and French beans in a pan of boiling salted water for 2 minutes. Drain and set aside on a tray.

2 Heat a drizzle of olive oil in a saucepan, add the spring onions, celery and potatoes, and fry for about 3 minutes until the spring onions are soft, stirring occasionally. Add the blanched vegetables and fry for a further 5 minutes.

3 Pour in the chicken stock. Bring to the boil, then simmer for 15 minutes.

4 Stir in the double cream and season with salt and pepper. Serve in bowls with a drizzle of fresh pesto on top.

1 tbsp extra virgin olive oil,
   plus extra for drizzling
4 celery sticks, finely chopped
2 small carrots, finely chopped
1 red onion, finely chopped
1 garlic clove, sliced
1 tsp chopped thyme
50g dried porcini mushrooms
1 x 400g can chopped tomatoes
1 tbsp chopped parsley
4 slices of ciabatta bread
1 garlic clove, cut in half
4 or 8 organic eggs
sea salt and freshly ground
   black pepper

I first ate Acqua Cotta in a trattoria in Montalcino. It was served on a big oval plate with a very generous helping of new season's olive oil. I had this version, with eggs, not far away a few years later and it was delicious. This will be enough to eat on its own as it is very filling. If you can get fresh porcini, use 200g, sliced. Poach the eggs separately, if you prefer. Serves 4 for lunch or supper.

acqua cotta

1 Heat the olive oil in a wide saucepan, add the chopped vegetables with the sliced garlic and thyme, and sweat down for 10–15 minutes until softened.

2 Meanwhile, soak the dried porcini in 100ml hot water until soft and rehydrated. Drain, reserving the soaking water.

3 Add the porcini to the vegetables in the pan and cook for a further 5 minutes, stirring occasionally.

4 Add the tomatoes, increase the heat and cook for 5 minutes, stirring occasionally. Pour in 500ml water and the reserved porcini soaking liquid and bring to a simmer. Add the parsley and season with salt and pepper. Leave to simmer for 5 minutes.

5 Toast the slices of ciabatta, then rub with the garlic halves and add a drizzle of olive oil. Rip up the toasted bread and add to the soup. It will be very thick.

6 Crack the eggs into the soup, leaving space between them. Cover and cook gently for 2–3 minutes until lightly poached. Serve in bowls.

3 organic eggs
2 tbsp milk
50g unsalted butter
100g goats' curd
1 tbsp lavender honey
sea salt and freshly ground
    black pepper
toasted sourdough bread,
    to serve

This may sound like an odd combination, but the creamy goats' curd goes so well with the honey. Don't make the omelette with aged goats' cheese because it will be too strong. Serves 2 for breakfast or brunch.

omelette
with goats' curd and lavender honey

1 Whisk the eggs in a bowl with the milk and season with salt and pepper.

2 Heat the butter in a 20cm non-stick frying pan until it foams. Pour in the beaten eggs. As they start to set, gently fold back the edges with a silicone spatula or wooden spoon so the uncooked egg can run on to the pan.

3 When the omelette is almost cooked, add the goats' curd and fold the omelette over in half.

4 Drizzle over the honey and serve at once with toasted sourdough bread.

15g unsalted butter
1 medium white onion, finely chopped
300g potatoes, peeled and cut into
   2cm pieces
1 bay leaf
600ml milk
1 whole kipper, preferably a Craster
   kipper, filleted and skinned
3 tbsp double cream
2 tbsp chopped parsley
sea salt and freshly ground
   black pepper

Cullen skink soup is traditionally made with smoked haddock but I find the sweet taste of kipper to be better. Ask your fishmonger to fillet and skin the kipper, or do this yourself, but take care when removing the pinbones to be sure you get them all. I find that warming the kipper first makes the bones come out more easily. Serves 4 as a starter or 2 for lunch.

kippers cullen skink

1 Melt the butter in a large heavy-based saucepan. Add the onion and cook until softened.

2 Add the potatoes, bay leaf and milk. Bring just to the boil, then simmer for 10–15 minutes until the potatoes are soft.

3 Meanwhile, check the kipper fillets for pinbones and remove any with tweezers, then flake the fillets into pieces. Add most of the kipper pieces to the saucepan and season with salt and pepper.

4 Blitz the soup roughly with a hand blender, then stir in the cream and most of the chopped parsley. Reheat if necessary and serve hot, garnished with the remaining kipper pieces and parsley.

25g dried porcini mushrooms
150g fresh spinach
2 tbsp extra virgin olive oil,
    plus extra for drizzling
1 garlic clove, sliced
1 x 400g can chopped plum tomatoes
1 tsp chopped thyme
1 x 400g jar or can chickpeas,
    drained (rinse if canned)
75g Parmesan cheese, freshly grated
sea salt and freshly ground black pepper

This is such an easy dish to make if you have a jar or can of chickpeas to hand. I've called it a stew rather than a soup because it is thick and chunky. Chickpeas from a jar will taste better than canned as they tend to be softer and creamier. Serves 4 as a starter or 2 for lunch.

porcini, chickpea and parmesan stew

1 Put the porcini in a small bowl, cover with 75ml boiling water and set aside to soak for 10–15 minutes until soft. Drain, reserving the soaking liquid.

2 While the porcini are soaking, blanch the spinach in a pan of boiling water until wilted. Drain and, when cool enough, squeeze or press out the excess liquid. Chop the spinach and set aside.

3 Heat a heavy-based saucepan, add the olive oil and garlic and cook until soft. Add the porcini, tomatoes and thyme, and cook for 10 minutes.

4 Add the chickpeas with 250ml water and the reserved porcini soaking liquid (leave any sediment behind in the bowl). Cook for another 10 minutes.

5 Add the chopped spinach and season with salt and pepper. Ladle the stew into bowls and top each with grated Parmesan and a drizzle of olive oil.

1kg ripe onion squash (or butternut squash)
1 small onion, finely chopped
100g pancetta cubes
1 tbsp extra virgin olive oil
1 tsp chopped thyme
300g Charlotte potatoes, peeled and cubed
1 litre fresh chicken stock (for home-made,
    see recipe on page 219)
2 tbsp crème fraîche
sea salt and freshly ground black pepper

This is a very comforting smooth soup.
A little crème fraîche stirred in at the end
just finishes it off. Try to use onion squash
as its flavour is better than butternut.
Serves 4–6 as a starter or 3–4 for lunch.

squash, pancetta and potato soup

1 Peel the squash and remove the seeds
and fibres. Cut the flesh into cubes.

2 Fry the onion and pancetta in the olive
oil in a heavy-based saucepan until light
gold in colour. Add the thyme, squash
and potatoes and stir, then cook for
a further 5 minutes.

3 Pour in the chicken stock and bring
to the boil. Reduce the heat and simmer
for 30 minutes.

4 Ladle into a blender and pulse until
smooth. Pour back into the pan and stir in
the crème fraîche and salt and pepper to
taste. Reheat if necessary before serving.

1 head of puntarelle, about 500g
1 garlic clove, peeled
½ tsp flaked sea salt
6 anchovy fillets (packed in oil), drained
1 tsp red wine vinegar
pinch of dried chilli flakes
5 tbsp extra virgin olive oil
1 tsp small capers in vinegar, drained
freshly ground black pepper

I start asking my supplier when the puntarelle is coming into season a good month before it does, as I am always keen to make this most delicious salad. The slightly bitter winter chicory with the anchovy, garlic and vinegar dressing is highly addictive. It's traditionally served as a side dish with fish or meat, but I like it as a starter. Only the tender puntarelle spears are eaten – the base or core is hard and woody and needs to be trimmed off. Italians are lucky enough to buy ready-prepared puntarelle in markets in season. Serves 2.

puntarelle

1 Remove any dark green leaves from the puntarelle, then cut the spears from the central core. Cut each spear lengthways into thin strips. Place them in a bowl of iced water and leave for 5 minutes, then remove and dry in a tea towel or salad spinner.

2 Make the dressing while the puntarelle is in the iced water. Pound the garlic with the salt using a mortar and pestle. Add the anchovies and pound to a paste. Add the vinegar and chilli flakes and pound to emulsify. Stir in the olive oil, then season with black pepper.

3 Put the puntarelle in a bowl. Add the dressing and capers and toss to mix, then serve.

100g Castelluccio or Puy lentils
250g fresh chicken livers
100g sliced pancetta
leaves from 1 sprig of sage
2 tbsp aged balsamic vinegar
4 tbsp extra virgin olive oil
1 lemon
250g mixed leaves, such as
    dandelion, radicchio, rocket
    or Castelfranco
sea salt and freshly ground
    black pepper

I like to use dandelion leaves in this warm salad. If you have some dandelions in your garden, don't just dig them up. As long as you haven't sprayed them with a pesticide, pick the young, tender leaves, which are pleasantly bitter. There's no need to blanch them by covering as they do in France. If you're worried about cats and foxes visiting your garden, just wash the leaves in a Milton solution. Serves 4 as a starter or 2 for supper.

warm chicken liver salad

1 Cook the lentils in a pan of simmering water for 20–25 minutes until soft.

2 Meanwhile, trim off any greenish bits and visible sinew from the chicken livers, then set aside. Cook the pancetta in a frying pan until crisp. Remove with tongs and set aside to drain on kitchen paper. Add the chicken livers to the fat remaining in the pan and cook for about 2 minutes on each side until golden brown all over. Remove from the heat.

3 Return the pancetta to the pan (don't worry if the slices break up) along with the sage leaves. Add 1 tablespoon balsamic vinegar and season with salt and pepper. Toss together, then set aside.

4 When the lentils are cooked, drain off the water. Add 1 tablespoon olive oil, a squeeze of lemon and seasoning.

5 In a large bowl, toss the leaves with the remaining balsamic vinegar and olive oil. Add the lentils and mix gently together.

6 Pile the lentils and leaves on the plates and place the chicken livers and pancetta carefully on top.

500g English asparagus
4 organic eggs
dash of vinegar
about 5 tbsp extra virgin olive oil
75g Parmesan cheese, freshly grated
shavings of fresh spring truffle (optional)
sea salt and freshly ground black pepper

The English asparagus season is always very exciting and I tend to eat an awful lot – the season is short so I put asparagus with everything. It's unbeatable with a good poached egg, some fresh Parmesan and a few shavings of an early summer truffle. Italian eggs have deeply coloured yolks, which look beautiful oozing out over asparagus. Here in the UK I recommend using Burford Brown eggs from Clarence Court, which have yolks of a similar rich colour. Serves 4 as a starter.

poached egg
with asparagus, parmesan and truffle

1 Snap off the tough ends from the asparagus spears, then peel the stalks to remove the tough outer skin. Cook the spears in a pan of simmering salted water for 4–5 minutes until tender. Lift out and drain on a tea towel. Keep hot.

2 While the asparagus is simmering, poach the eggs for 2–3 minutes in a wide pan of boiling salted water with a dash of vinegar. Carefully remove them with a slotted spoon and lay them on a tea towel to drain.

3 Lay the asparagus spears on plates and season each serving with a dash of olive oil and some salt and pepper. Place the poached eggs on top. Scatter Parmesan over the plates and add some truffle shavings, if using. Finish with a twist of black pepper and a drizzle of olive oil.

1 tbsp extra virgin olive oil
5 slices smoked ham, roughly torn
4 organic eggs
crusty sourdough bread, to serve

For the peperonata
3 tbsp extra virgin olive oil
½ red onion, sliced
1 red pepper, seeded and sliced
1 yellow pepper, seeded and sliced
1 fresh red chilli, seeded and sliced
1 garlic clove, sliced
1 x 400g can chopped tomatoes
1 tsp small capers in vinegar, drained
sea salt and freshly ground black pepper

I make this a lot because my daughter loves peperonata – when she was little she would always call it 'red stuff' and that name has stuck in our family. Make sure you cut the peppers finely and cook them slowly. The longer you cook peperonata, the better it tastes. Serves 2 for brunch or supper.

eggs peperonata
with smoked ham

1 First make the peperonata. Heat the olive oil in a large frying pan on a medium heat. Add the onion and fry gently for 3–4 minutes until translucent, then stir in the peppers, chilli and garlic. Cook on a low heat for 20 minutes until the vegetables are softened, stirring occasionally.

2 Tip in the tomatoes. Increase the heat to medium and simmer gently for 10 minutes until the sauce has thickened. Season with salt and pepper and stir in the capers.

3 While the peperonata is simmering, prepare the ham and eggs. Heat the olive oil in a large frying pan on a medium heat, add the ham and fry for 2–3 minutes until lightly browned in places. Turn the heat down to medium-low and crack the eggs on top of the ham. Cook for a further 3–4 minutes until the eggs are cooked to your liking.

4 Spoon the eggs and ham on top of the pepperonata. Add a grinding of pepper and serve straight from the pan with some crusty sourdough bread.

50g dried porcini mushrooms
50ml extra virgin olive oil
1 garlic clove, chopped
200g portobello mushrooms, sliced
   (or fresh girolles and trompettes
   de mort, if available)
3 organic eggs
100ml double cream
50g unsalted butter
sprig of parsley, chopped
100g ricotta cheese
75g Parmesan cheese, freshly grated
sea salt and freshly ground black pepper

The Italian open or flat omelettes called frittatas may be light or more substantial and can be served hot or cold. This frittata is a really good winter one with the addition of porcini and portobello mushrooms and ricotta. Serves 2 for lunch.

frittata con funghi

1 Put the dried porcini in a bowl, pour over 100 ml of boiling water to cover and set aside to soak.

2 Meanwhile, heat a large heavy-based saucepan. Add the olive oil and garlic and cook for 1 minute. Add the portobello mushrooms and cook, stirring occasionally, for about 10 minutes until the mushrooms are dark and all the moisture from them has evaporated.

3 Squeeze out the porcini mushrooms (reserve the soaking liquid), then add to the pan and stir into the portobello mushrooms. Add the soaking liquid, leaving any sediment behind in the bowl, and cook for a further 5 minutes. Season with salt and pepper, then set aside.

4 Preheat the grill to high. Whisk the eggs with the cream in a bowl, just to mix. Heat a small ovenproof frying pan (about 20cm diameter) and add the butter. When the butter is foaming, pour in the egg mix and beat with a fork, then let the eggs set on the base.

5 Spoon the mushrooms, chopped parsley, ricotta and Parmesan over the eggs. Place the pan under the grill and cook for a minute or so to set the top of the frittata. Serve hot.

2 red peppers
1 loaf of dry ciabatta bread
300g heritage tomatoes,
   preferably of mixed colours
1 heaped tsp small capers
   in vinegar, drained
a few anchovy fillets
   (packed in oil), drained

For the dressing
400g ripe plum tomatoes
1 garlic clove, peeled
sea salt
5 anchovy fillets
   (packed in oil), drained
small bunch of basil
150ml extra virgin olive oil
2 tsp red wine vinegar
1 heaped tsp small capers
   in vinegar, drained

I don't know anyone who doesn't love this salad. It's a traditional Italian way to use up leftover bread. There are other versions, but this is a very simple way to make it. If you only have very soft, fresh bread, try baking it for a few minutes to harden it – then it will absorb the dressing without going soggy. Serves 4 as a starter.

panzanella

1 Preheat a hot grill, then char the red peppers on all sides. Put them in a bowl and cover with clingfilm. Leave to cool for 10 minutes before scraping off the charred skin with a serrated knife. Rinse off the seeds, then rip the peppers into 1cm strips. Set aside.

2 Make the dressing while the peppers are cooling in the bowl. Score the skins of the tomatoes, then put them into a pan of boiling water and leave to blanch for 1 minute. Lift into a bowl of cold water with a slotted spoon, then peel off the skins. Crush the garlic with 1 teaspoon sea salt using a pestle and mortar until smooth. Add the anchovies and half the basil, pounding to a paste. Squeeze the peeled tomatoes to a pulp, then add to the

garlic and anchovies. Add the olive oil, red wine vinegar and capers. Mix well together.

3 Remove the crusts from the ciabatta, then cut into 2cm pieces. Put them in a large salad bowl and add the grilled peppers. Pour over the anchovy and tomato dressing and toss well so the bread can soak up all the dressing.

4 Roughly cut up the heritage tomatoes and toss with the rest of the basil leaves in a separate bowl. Spread the tomatoes and basil over the top of the salad, then add the capers and a few whole anchovy fillets. Clean up the sides of the bowl before serving.

1kg Maris Piper potatoes
100g sliced pancetta
2 tbsp extra virgin olive oil
white wine vinegar
2 duck eggs
sea salt and freshly ground
    black pepper

For the sauce
2 tbsp extra virgin olive oil
1 garlic clove, sliced
1 small, dried bird's eye chilli,
    seeded and chopped
1 tsp dried oregano
1 x 400g can chopped
    plum tomatoes

I first had a rösti potato on a school skiing trip to Switzerland and have loved them ever since. The pizzaiola sauce – a basic tomato sauce with oregano – works really well with the crisp rösti topped with poached eggs and pancetta. Serves 2 as a starter or for lunch.

rosti potato
with eggs and pizzaiola sauce

1 First make the sauce. Heat the olive oil in a heavy-based saucepan, add the garlic, chilli and oregano, and cook for 1 minute. Stir in the chopped tomatoes and cook over a low heat for 15 minutes, stirring occasionally. Keep warm until ready to serve.

2 While the sauce is simmering, peel the potatoes, then coarsely grate them into a colander. In handfuls, squeeze out as much moisture from the grated potatoes as you can and discard it, then put the potatoes in a bowl. Season the potatoes with salt and pepper to taste.

3 Cook the pancetta in a large, non-stick frying pan until crisp. Remove from the pan and set aside to drain on kitchen paper.

4 Add the olive oil to the pancetta fat left in the pan and heat until smoking, then add the grated potatoes and push down evenly to form a large cake. Cook for 5–7 minutes until golden brown on the base, then flip over and cook for another 5–7 minutes. Transfer to a large, warmed plate and keep hot.

5 Bring a pan of salted water to the boil and add a dash of vinegar. Crack the eggs into the water and poach for about 3 minutes until just cooked.

6 Lift out the poached eggs and drain briefly on kitchen paper, then place on the potato rösti. Add the cooked pancetta and drizzle the sauce over the top. Serve immediately.

pasta, gnocchi and risottos

For me, a plate of pasta or risotto, made with the very best quality ingredients, is unbeatable. Both pasta and rice can be combined with a wide variety of other foods and flavourings, to make a dish that is part of a meal or the main event. Here in the UK we tend to cook pasta and risotto as a main meal, whereas the Italian way is to serve a starter portion – everyone licks their plate and wishes there was more, but within 10 minutes of digesting they realise they have eaten enough without feeling really full and fat! In this chapter I give you pastas, gnocchi and risottos that can be served as starters or that are enough to make a good supper. For the best results, cook them when their key ingredients are in season.

300g asparagus
250g dried linguine
3 organic egg yolks
1 garlic clove, crushed with
   a pinch of sea salt
100g Parmesan cheese, freshly
   grated, plus extra for serving
sea salt and freshly ground
   black pepper

Asparagus is the most delicious springtime vegetable and there are so many ways to serve it. I love eating it like this. The pasta water is added to thin down the egg yolks. If you used cream instead, as in a normal Carbonara, the dish would be too heavy and the asparagus not be as appetising. Serves 2 as a starter.

asparagus carbonara
with linguine

1 Snap off the tough ends of the asparagus spears, then cut at an angle into 1cm slices. Keep to one side.

2 Cook the linguine in a pot of boiling salted water until just al dente (this will be about 2 minutes less than the cooking time on the packet).

3 Meanwhile, put the egg yolks and garlic into a sauté pan (off the heat) and beat just until the yolks are broken up. Add a few spoons of the pasta water and keep to one side.

4 When the pasta has been cooking for about 5 minutes, add the asparagus to the pot. Continue cooking until the pasta is ready.

5 Using a large metal sieve, remove the linguine and sliced asparagus from the pot and add to the sauté pan. Add the Parmesan. Set the pan on a medium heat and toss the pasta by shaking the pan, or using a wooden spoon, so that a sauce forms and coats the strands of pasta nicely. Add a few more spoonfuls of the pasta water if the sauce is a bit too thick.

6 Serve with more Parmesan and freshly ground black pepper.

200g dried linguine
5 tbsp extra virgin olive oil
1 garlic clove, finely sliced
8 Taggiasche or small niçoise olives, pitted
10 cherry tomatoes, each cut into quarters
2 red mullet fillets
1 tsp chopped flat-leaf parsley

For the pangratatto
200ml sunflower oil
100g stale bread, roughly chopped
   into coarse crumbs
sea salt and freshly ground black pepper

Red mullet is one of my favourite fish. It has a flavour like no other, probably because of its natural sweet fat. The trick to this recipe is to melt the tomatoes, olives and garlic rather than fry them, and to use the heat of the pasta to cook the red mullet. That way you get the best out of your ingredients. The pangratatto (crisp-fried coarse crumbs of bread) adds a lovely texture that is very welcome when you are eating this dish. Serves 2 for lunch or supper.

linguine with red mullet,
tomatoes, olives and pangratatto

1 For the pangratatto, heat the sunflower oil in a deep pan to 160°C. Add the breadcrumbs and deep-fry until golden brown. Drain on kitchen paper and sprinkle with salt. Set aside.

2 Cook the linguine in a large pot of boiling salted water until just al dente (about 2 minutes less than the cooking time on the packet).

3 Meanwhile, heat a frying pan and add 3 tablespoons olive oil, then add the garlic, black olives and cherry tomatoes. These should melt rather than fry. After a couple of minutes add the red mullet fillets and chopped parsley. Season with salt and pepper. Remove from the heat for the moment, until the pasta is ready.

4 When the pasta is just al dente, take it out with tongs and add to the frying pan. (If the red mullet still looks raw when you add the pasta, don't worry – the heat of the pasta will cook the fillets as they are very delicate.) Toss the pasta with the other ingredients in the pan (the fish will break up).

5 Place the pan on a low heat. Add a spoonful or two of the pasta water and the remaining olive oil, and check the seasoning, then toss so the starch is released from the pasta and the sauce becomes emulsified. Serve hot, with the pangrattato scattered on top.

3 tbsp extra virgin olive oil
1 shallot, finely chopped
5 slices pancetta, cut into strips
1 garlic clove, chopped
4 sage leaves, chopped
1 small, ripe onion squash, peeled,
    seeded and cut into 1cm pieces
150g cooked cannellini beans
    (or from a jar, well drained)
250g dried spirale pasta
freshly grated Parmesan cheese, to serve
sea salt and freshly ground black pepper

This is a dish for autumn because from September you can buy onion squash that is ripe and full of sweet flavour. A lot of the squash you buy isn't ripe – it has been picked too early and thus has not benefited from being left on the plant to mature fully. You can tell by the colour of the skin and the flesh: if there are any traces of green or the squash is slightly bitter or very starchy, then it is not ripe. (I always buy a few squashes and leave them to ripen on a windowsill.) I put cannellini beans in this recipe because they bring all the flavours together and make this dish more substantial. If you are making this after November, be sure to finish it with a drizzle of the green, new season's Tuscan olive oil.
Serves 2 for lunch.

spirale pasta
with onion squash, pancetta
and cannellini beans

1 Heat 2 tablespoons of olive oil in a sauté pan and fry the shallot, pancetta, garlic and sage until the pancetta is a light golden colour. Add the squash pieces along with 3 tablespoons water and a pinch of salt. Place the lid on the pan and cook gently for 10 minutes until the squash is soft.

2 Add the cannellini beans and stir to mix, then leave on a low heat to keep warm.

3 Cook the pasta in a pot of boiling salted water until just al dente. Using a slotted spoon, transfer the pasta to the sauté pan and add 3 tablespoons of the pasta water. Toss well. Check the seasoning and add the remaining olive oil. Finish with some freshly grated Parmesan cheese.

200g fresh clams (palourde) in shells
3 tbsp extra virgin olive oil
1 garlic clove, finely chopped
50ml dry white wine
100g fresh swordfish fillets,
    cut into small pieces
4 large raw prawns, peeled
    and cut into 1cm pieces
6 cherry tomatoes, each cut into quarters
1 tbsp chopped flat-leaf parsley
250g fresh or dried pappardelle pasta
sea salt and freshly ground black pepper

This wide pasta is normally served with a meat sauce, but I find that the clams, prawns and swordfish sit nicely on top of the pappardelle and the pasta absorbs their juices. Serve this on large warm plates so the pappardelle isn't piled up too much. Then the sauce will be evenly distributed. Serves 2 for supper.

pappardelle with clams,
prawns and swordfish

1 Put the clams in a colander and rinse thoroughly under cold running water, shaking the colander vigorously. Discard any clams that remain open.

2 Heat a frying pan. Add 1 tablespoon olive oil and then the clams. Place a lid on top and cook for 30 seconds. Add the garlic and white wine and shake the pan to mix and redistribute the clams, then put the lid back on and cook until the clams have opened. Discard any that remain closed.

3 Add the swordfish, prawns, cherry tomatoes and parsley. Remove from the heat.

4 Cook the pappardelle in a pot of boiling salted water until just al dente.

5 Lift the pasta out of the pan with a pair of tongs and add to the frying pan along with a couple of spoonfuls of the pasta water. Cook for a couple of minutes, tossing the ingredients together so the starch from the pasta starts to thicken the sauce.

6 Check and adjust the seasoning and add the remaining olive oil, then toss together one more time before serving.

100g trimmed samphire
2 large cleaned scallops
6 medium raw prawns, peeled
2 tbsp extra virgin olive oil
1 garlic clove, thinly sliced
4 Datterini or cherry tomatoes,
   each cut into quarters
2 tbsp crème fraîche
250g fresh or dried tagliarini pasta
sea salt and freshly ground
   black pepper

If you can use fresh scallops from the shell, this dish will taste even better. Cut them in rounds so you can tell they are scallops. Their sweetness works well with the prawns and salty samphire. The addition of crème fraîche is unusual, but it brings all the flavours together and dresses the tagliarini well. Serves 2 for lunch.

tagliarini
with scallops, prawns and samphire

1 Blanch the samphire in boiling water for 1 minute; drain.

2 Cut each scallop horizontally into three discs. Cut each prawn into three pieces. Toss the scallops and prawns in the olive oil and season with salt and pepper.

3 Heat a non-stick frying pan and sear the prawns and scallops so they take on a little colour. Add the garlic and tomatoes and cook for 1 minute, then stir in the crème fraîche and samphire. Remove from the heat and keep warm.

4 Cook the tagliarini in a pot of boiling salted water until al dente. Using tongs, remove the pasta from the water and add to the frying pan, along with a few spoonfuls of the pasta water. Toss well to mix. Season with black pepper and possibly a bit of salt but be careful as the samphire can be salty. Serve immediately.

For the pasta
250g tipo 00 flour
25g fine semolina flour,
  plus extra for dusting
1 whole organic egg
6 organic egg yolks

For the sauce
2 courgettes
200g cleaned fresh squid,
  with tentacles
2 tbsp extra virgin olive oil
8 Datterini or other small
  tomatoes, peeled
1 garlic clove, finely chopped
1 tsp chopped flat-leaf parsley
pinch of dried chilli flakes
20g bottarga, shaved
sea salt and freshly ground
  black pepper

tagliatelle with squid,
courgettes, tomatoes and bottarga

You need small tender squid for this recipe. The sauce is made by briefly cooking the squid with tomatoes, parsley and garlic in olive oil. Then you add the cooked tagliatelle and courgettes, at which point a lot of juice is released. So make sure you toss the pasta well – its starch will emulsify everything together. Bottarga is the roe from a grey mullet that has been salted and dried. It has a very distinctive flavour and works brilliantly in this dish as a seasoning. Serves 4 as a starter or 2 for supper.

1 To make the pasta, put all the ingredients into a food processor and pulse until well combined and the mixture comes together into a dough. Transfer the dough to a bowl, cover with clingfilm and leave to rest in the fridge for 30 minutes.

2 Cut the pasta dough in half and feed one of the pieces through a pasta machine, following the machine instructions, starting with the rollers on their widest setting and ending on the thinnest setting. Add the tagliatelle cutter to the pasta machine, then pass the rolled sheet of pasta through to make thin strips. Repeat the process with the remaining dough.

recipe continues overleaf

tagliatelle with squid, courgettes, tomatoes and bottarga *continued*

3 Dust the tagliatelle with semolina flour, to keep the strands separate, then place on a plate. If not using immediately, cover and keep in the fridge overnight.

4 For the sauce, very finely slice the courgettes using a mandoline, then cut into strips the same size as the tagliatelle. Cut each squid body in half lengthways and open out flat, skinned side down. Score with a sharp knife in a criss-cross pattern, then cut into strips the same size as the courgettes and tagliatelle.

5 Bring a large pot of salted water to the boil. Add the tagliatelle and courgettes, bring back to the boil and cook for 2 minutes.

6 Meanwhile, heat a frying pan until medium hot, then add the olive oil, squid, tomatoes, garlic and parsley and cook gently for 2 minutes.

7 Using tongs, transfer the pasta and courgettes to the frying pan and toss thoroughly to mix with the other ingredients. Season with the chilli flakes, salt and pepper. Serve immediately, with the bottarga scattered on top.

super quick **35 minutes** a little more time leisurely but worth it
quick

250g fresh tagliatelle
2 courgettes, cut into long strips

For the pesto
1 garlic clove, peeled
150g basil leaves
75g pine nuts, preferably Mediterranean
100g Parmesan cheese, freshly grated
5 tbsp extra virgin olive oil
sea salt and freshly ground black pepper

Pesto is very easy to make and brings out the best of fresh basil. It works perfectly with courgettes, and together they make the tagliatelle juicy and flavoursome. Serves 2 as a starter or for lunch.

tagliatelle with pesto
and courgettes

1 First make the pesto. Using a pestle and mortar, crush the garlic with ½ teaspoon sea salt to a smooth paste. Add the basil leaves and pound so the leaves turn to a pulp. Add the pine nuts and crush until smooth. Add 3 tablespoons water and emulsify, then add the Parmesan cheese. Finally, slowly work in the olive oil.

2 Cook the pasta with the courgettes in a large pot of boiling salted water for about 3 minutes – the pasta should still have a bite.

3 Meanwhile, warm half the pesto in a frying pan.

4 Using tongs, lift the pasta and courgettes from the water and add to the frying pan. Toss with the pesto and add 2–3 tablespoons of the pasta water to loosen the sauce so it coats the pasta strands.

5 Check and adjust the seasoning and serve with the remaining pesto on top.

1 litre full-fat milk
freshly grated nutmeg
225g fine semolina
3 organic egg yolks
100g unsalted butter
150g Parmesan cheese,
    freshly grated
sea salt and freshly ground
    black pepper

This is definitely comfort food and is brilliant to serve to children because of its size and flavour. If you happen to have a white truffle, shave some on top. Serves 3–4 as a starter.

gnocchi alla romana

1 Pour the milk into a heavy-based saucepan and bring to a gentle simmer. Grate in about an eighth of a nutmeg. Whisk the semolina into the milk, whisking quickly to prevent any lumps from forming. The mixture should be thick and smooth. Keep cooking on a low heat, whisking occasionally, for about 15 minutes until the mixture starts to come away from the sides of the pan.

2 Whisking vigorously, add the egg yolks. When they are absorbed into the mixture add half the butter and 50g of the Parmesan and mix well. Then add the remaining butter and another 50g of the Parmesan and whisk so that all the ingredients are incorporated and the mixture is smooth. Season.

3 Pour the semolina mixture on to a buttered tray in a 2cm-thick layer. Leave to cool, then chill in the fridge for 10 minutes.

4 Preheat the oven to 190°C. Using a 4cm round cutter, or a Champagne flute, cut out as many discs from the semolina mixture as you can. Place them on a well-buttered baking sheet, leaving a 2cm gap between each disc.

5 Sprinkle the remaining Parmesan on top of the gnocchi, then bake for 10 minutes until they have all puffed up like a soufflé and are a light golden brown. Serve immediately.

**45 minutes,
plus chilling time**
leisurely but worth it

400g fresh spinach,
   washed thoroughly
150g fresh ricotta
100g Parmesan cheese, freshly
   grated, plus extra for serving
2 organic egg yolks
75g tipo 00 flour
50g unsalted butter
4 sage leaves
sea salt and freshly ground
   black pepper

I have been making this dish for years and have changed it a few times. There are no potatoes in the mix, which means the gnocchi are extra light. Just be sure not to add any more flour than you need – too much will make the gnocchi heavy and the overpowering flavour will be flour. Serves 2 as a starter or for lunch.

gnocchi with spinach,
ricotta, parmesan and sage butter

1 Cook the spinach in a pan of boiling salted water just until the stems are soft. Drain in a colander. When cool enough to handle, squeeze out any excess water, then chop finely.

2 Put the spinach in a large bowl and add the ricotta, Parmesan, egg yolks and flour. Mix together well, seasoning with salt and pepper.

3 Using two tablespoons, take a walnut-size piece of the gnocchi mix and scoop the spoons together to create an even oval shape like an egg (just as you do when shaping a quenelle). Tip the shaped gnoccho on to a greaseproof-lined tray. Repeat until you have used all of the mixture. Chill in the fridge for 1 hour.

4 Heat a frying pan, then add the butter and melt it. Add the sage leaves. Keep warm.

5 Bring a pot of salted water to the boil. Lower in the gnocchi carefully, reduce the heat and simmer gently until they rise to the surface. Take them out, a few at a time, with a slotted spoon and tap the spoon on a tea towel to absorb any excess water before placing them in the frying pan with the sage butter. Spoon the warm butter over them to coat all over.

6 Serve on hot starter plates or in pasta bowls with extra freshly grated Parmesan and black pepper.

2 medium globe artichokes
juice of 1 lemon
1 tbsp extra virgin olive oil
1 garlic clove, sliced
½ tsp chopped thyme
50g unsalted butter
75g Parmesan cheese,
    freshly grated
freshly ground black pepper

For the gnocchi
500g floury potatoes such
    as Maris Piper, peeled
    and cut in half
100g tipo 00 flour,
    plus extra for dusting
1 organic egg, beaten

gnocchi
with globe artichokes and parmesan

Potato gnocchi are very easy to make. Just be careful how much flour you use: the more you add, the heavier the gnocchi will be. Potato gnocchi should be light. Serves 4 as a starter or 2 for supper.

1 To make the gnocchi, cook the potatoes in boiling salted water until soft. Drain, then return to the empty pan, cover it with a tea towel and leave for a few minutes to make sure the steam evaporates. Press the potatoes through a mouli-légumes or potato ricer into a large bowl. Leave to cool.

2 Add the flour and egg to the smoothly mashed potato and mix to form a soft dough. Divide into three pieces. Using the palms of your hands and your fingertips, roll each piece on a lightly floured worktop into a long sausage about 2cm in diameter. Cut into 2cm lengths. Gently press each length over the back of a fork, then drop on to the floured surface. (Pressing on the fork gives the gnocchi a few ridges and a crevice, which will help to hold the sauce and make them really tasty.) Set aside.

3 Next prepare the artichokes, one at a time. First fill a large bowl with water and add the lemon juice (or a handful of parsley stalks, which will do the same job). Remove the tough outer leaves from the artichoke, then cut off the top to expose the furry choke surrounded by tender inner leaves. Use a teaspoon to scoop out the choke. Remove the tough, stringy outer part of the stem to leave just the tender core, and trim the end. Cut the artichoke lengthways in half and then cut each half lengthways into 5mm slices. Without delay, immerse the artichoke slices in the lemon water solution to prevent them from turning brown.

4 Heat the olive oil in a frying pan with the garlic and thyme. Add the artichokes and 100ml of cold water. Cover and cook for about 5 minutes until the artichoke slices are tender. Remove from the heat and add the butter. Keep warm while you cook the gnocchi.

5 Slip the gnocchi into a pot of boiling salted water and cook until they rise to the surface. Carefully remove them with a slotted spoon and add to the frying pan along with a few spoonfuls of the cooking water. Toss gently with the artichokes, then add the Parmesan and toss well until you get a really creamy consistency. Finish with a good grinding of black pepper before serving.

100g unsalted butter
2 spring onions, chopped
200g Carnaroli risotto rice
½ glass of white wine
1 litre hot, fresh chicken stock
    (for home-made, see recipe
    on page 219)
200g shelled fresh peas
5 mint leaves, chopped
150g Parmesan cheese, freshly
    grated, plus shavings to finish
150g sliced prosciutto di Parma,
    roughly torn
sea salt and freshly ground
    black pepper

If you can get fresh peas then use them in this risotto. When they're out of season, frozen petit pois will work well. Just make sure you blanch them first for a minute and add nearer the end of the cooking time. The prosciutto is used like a seasoning and gives the risotto a richer flavour. Serves 4 as a starter or 2 for supper.

risotto with peas,
prosciutto and parmesan

1 Melt half the butter in a heavy-based saucepan and sweat the spring onions on a low heat until soft. Add the rice and stir for 5 minutes until translucent.

2 Add the white wine, turn up the heat and stir until it has almost all evaporated. Add one ladle of hot stock along with the peas and mint, and bubble, stirring, until the liquid has almost all been absorbed. Continue adding stock, little by little, stirring constantly and letting each addition be absorbed before adding more. When cooked the rice should still have a bite but no a crunch.

3 Add the Parmesan, the rest of the butter and the prosciutto with salt and pepper to taste. Stir until the risotto is creamy. Serve topped with shavings of Parmesan cheese.

juice of 1 lemon
8 globe artichokes
3 tbsp extra virgin olive oil
1 garlic clove, sliced
1 tbsp chopped red onion
1 tbsp chopped celery
200g Carnaroli risotto rice
½ glass of white wine
1 litre hot, fresh chicken stock
   (for home-made, see recipe page 219)
1 tbsp chopped parsley
50g unsalted butter
100g Parmesan cheese, freshly grated
sea salt and freshly ground black pepper

The great thing about a risotto is that you do not need much of an ingredient to flavour the rice. Try to use the small violet artichokes for this recipe as they are young and tender and there's little wastage. Always serve risotto from the pan so it is piping hot. Risotto waits for nobody! Serves 4 as a starter or 2 for supper.

artichoke risotto

1 First fill a large bowl with water and add some lemon juice (or parsley stalks, which will do the same job), then prepare the artichokes one at a time. Remove the tough outer leaves to reveal the pale inner heart. Cut off the stem close to the base. Open the inner heart and, using a teaspoon, scoop out the hairy choke. Cut the artichoke heart lengthways into eight. Without delay, immerse in the lemon water solution to prevent the artichoke pieces from turning brown.

2 Heat 1 tablespoon olive oil in a pan and add the drained artichokes with the garlic, 150ml water and some salt and pepper. Cover and cook for 5 minutes until tender. Set aside.

3 Heat the remaining olive oil in a large heavy-based saucepan and soften the onion and celery on a low heat. Add the rice and stir for 5 minutes until translucent.

4 Increase the heat and add the wine. Cook, stirring, until it has almost all been absorbed. Then start adding the hot stock, little by little, stirring continuously and letting each addition be absorbed before adding more. The finished risotto should be creamy, not set and heavy, and the rice still with a bite but no a crunch.

5 Stir in the artichokes with their cooking juices, the parsley, butter and Parmesan, and season with a squeeze of lemon, salt and pepper. Serve hot.

1 tbsp chopped red onion
1 tbsp chopped celery
1 tbsp extra virgin olive oil
75g pancetta cubes
1 tsp chopped rosemary,
   plus extra to garnish
200g Carnaroli risotto rice
1 litre hot, fresh chicken stock
   (for home-made, see recipe
   on page 219)
100g vacuum-packed peeled
   cooked chestnuts, finely chopped
2 shots of brandy
75g unsalted butter
100g Parmesan cheese, freshly grated
freshly ground black pepper

When chestnuts come into season, this is always the first thing I make with them. They have a starchy sweet taste that goes really well with pancetta and rosemary (always use fresh rosemary!). Serves 4 as a starter.

chestnut risotto

1 In a large heavy-based saucepan, soften the onion and celery in the olive oil with the pancetta and rosemary on a low heat. Add the rice and cook, stirring, for 5 minutes until translucent.

2 Turn up the heat and start adding the hot stock, little by little, stirring continuously and letting each addition be absorbed before adding more. After about 15 minutes, add the chestnuts and brandy, then continue adding the stock and cooking for 5 minutes. When cooked the rice should still have a bite but no crunch.

3 Add the butter and Parmesan and season with black pepper, then stir until the risotto is creamy. Serve hot, garnished with a few picked rosemary tips.

6 small courgettes with their
  flowers attached
2 tbsp extra virgin olive oil
1 garlic clove, sliced
1 tsp finely chopped onion
1 tsp finely chopped celery
200g Carnaroli risotto rice
½ glass of white wine
1 litre hot, fresh chicken stock
  (for home-made, see recipe
  on page 219)
75g unsalted butter
100g Parmesan cheese, freshly grated
1 heaped tbsp roughly torn basil leaves
sea salt and freshly ground black pepper

This is a great summer risotto. The main flavour is the courgettes, but the flowers give the risotto a lovely texture and also make it look very appetising. A generous addition of freshly grated Parmesan cheese to the risotto just before you serve it is very important. Serves 4 as a starter.

risotto
with courgette flowers

1 Separate the courgettes and their flowers; set the flowers aside. Slice the courgettes into thin rounds. Cook them in 1 tablespoon olive oil with the garlic for about 5 minutes until tender. Set aside.

2 Heat the remaining olive oil in a large heavy-based saucepan. Add the onion and celery and cook on a low heat for 3–4 minutes until soft. Add the rice and stir for 5 minutes until translucent.

3 Add the white wine, turn up the heat and cook until the wine has almost all evaporated. Start adding the hot stock, little by little, stirring continuously and letting each addition be absorbed before adding more. When cooked, the rice should still have a bite but no crunch.

4 Add the cooked courgettes along with their flowers, roughly torn, the butter, Parmesan and basil. Season with salt and pepper. Give the risotto a good final stir so it is really creamy, then serve.

2 tbsp extra virgin olive oil
1 tbsp chopped red onion
1 tbsp chopped celery
200g Carnaroli risotto rice
½ glass of white wine
1 litre hot, fresh chicken stock
    (for home-made, see recipe
    on page 219)
1 tbsp chopped parsley
50g unsalted butter
100g Parmesan cheese, freshly grated
sea salt and freshly ground black pepper

For the tomato sauce
500g ripe plum tomatoes
4 tbsp extra virgin olive oil
2 garlic cloves, sliced
10 basil leaves

I used to make this risotto for my children when they were little. It is so simple and little ones love it because it is smooth and almost sweet in flavour. You can use canned plum tomatoes or jarred passata for this, but in the summer use fresh, ripe tomatoes for the best taste. Serves 4 as a starter.

tomato risotto

1 Start with the tomato sauce. Score the skins of the tomatoes, then put them into a pan of boiling water and leave to blanch for 1 minute. Remove with a slotted spoon and place in a bowl of cold water. When cool enough to handle, peel the tomatoes, then remove the seeds and finely chop the flesh.

2 Heat the olive oil in a large saucepan and fry the garlic briefly. Add the chopped tomatoes and 8 of the basil leaves. Cook, stirring occasionally, for about 10 minutes until the sauce has thickened consistency.

3 Meanwhile, to make the risotto, heat the olive oil in a large heavy-based saucepan and soften the onion and celery on a low heat. Add the rice and cook, stirring, for 5 minutes.

4 Add the wine, increase the heat and stir until it has almost all evaporated. Now start adding the hot stock, little by little, stirring continuously and letting each addition be absorbed before adding more. When cooked the rice should still have a bite but no a crunch.

5 When the risotto is almost ready, add the tomato sauce, parsley, butter and Parmesan, and season with salt and pepper. Stir well until the risotto is creamy. Garnish with the remaining basil leaves, roughly torn, and serve hot.

1kg fresh clams (palourde) in shells
1 garlic clove, sliced
2 tsp chopped parsley
1 glass of white wine
2 tbsp extra virgin olive oil,
   plus extra to finish
1 small red onion, finely chopped
1 celery stick, finely chopped
200g Carnaroli risotto rice
1 litre hot, fresh fish stock (for home-
   made, see recipe on page 220)
2 red mullet fillets (skin scaled),
   each cut into 4 pieces
250g peeled, cooked brown shrimps
1 whole cooked lobster tail,
   cut across into quarters
3 tbsp tomato passata
sea salt and freshly ground
   black pepper

The most important element of this dish is the fish stock – the rice will be a bit dull without a strong flavoursome stock. Wait to add the fish until the last 5 minutes of cooking so it almost poaches in the stock. That way you will keep the chunky texture instead of having broken-up pieces of fish that will make the risotto really thick and heavy. Serves 4 for supper.

seafood risotto

1 Put the clams in a colander and rinse thoroughly under cold running water, shaking the colander vigorously. Discard any clams that remain open. Tip the clams into a large pan and add the garlic and half the parsley and wine. Cover and steam until the clam shells open. Remove from the heat and set aside. Discard any clams that remain closed.

2 While the clams are steaming, heat the olive oil in a large heavy-based saucepan and fry the onion and celery on a low heat until softened. Add the rice and cook for 5 minutes, stirring, until translucent.

3 Add the remaining white wine, increase the heat and cook until it has almost all evaporated, stirring constantly. Start adding the hot stock, little by little, stirring continuously and letting each addition be absorbed before adding more. When cooked the rice should still have a bite but no crunch.

4 When the risotto is almost ready, add the red mullet and cook for 2 minutes before adding the clams (with all their juices), brown shrimps and lobster. Add the tomato passata, remaining parsley, seasoning and a dash of olive oil. Stir thoroughly until everything is incorporated and the risotto is creamy. Serve in pasta bowls.

large plates
for sharing

I think, as a nation, we tend to be
slightly selfish when it comes to eating
out. In a restaurant we all get a starter,
a main course and then a dessert and
happily eat them without offering a
taste to anyone else. But at home we
can share, helping ourselves from large
plates in the middle of the table. I love
cooking these dishes and serving them
like this, with some side dishes, even if
there are only two of you, because it looks
impressive and seems more generous.
Somehow it adds enjoyment to the meal,
and it's more relaxing for the cook too.

300g Charlotte potatoes, peeled
2 globe artichokes
3 tbsp extra virgin olive oil,
   plus extra to finish
2 monkfish fillets, about 160g each
1 tbsp small capers in vinegar, drained
2 tsp chopped parsley
½ garlic clove, chopped
½ glass of white wine
100g sliced prosciutto di Parma
½ lemon
sea salt

When I first started as a Commis Chef many years ago, monkfish was quite cheap. It is now so expensive and sometimes disappointing. When buying it try to get day-boat fish as opposed to dredged fish. The difference is unbelievable! Dredged fish is usually drowned in the net, which means the fish has swallowed saltwater – this 'cures' the flesh, making it very white and wet and smelling of ammonia. Day-boat fish is caught in a more sustainable manner and its flesh will be firm and slightly translucent with a sweet flavour and no strong aroma. Serves 2.

monkfish
with prosciutto, capers, parsley and charlotte potatoes

1 Preheat the oven to 180°C. Cook the potatoes in a pan of boiling salted water for about 20 minutes until just tender. Drain and, when cool enough to handle, cut into 1cm slices.

2 While the potatoes are cooking, prepare the artichokes. Peel the stems to remove all the tough fibrous outside, then cook the artichokes whole in another pan of boiling salted water for about 15 minutes until tender: you should be able to put a knife through the stem and heart of the artichoke with ease. Drain. Peel off the outer leaves, then cut off the top and scoop out the choke. Quarter each artichoke lengthways.

3 Heat the olive oil in a large ovenproof frying pan and sear the monkfish fillets on one side until golden brown. Turn them over and sear the other side. Remove.

4 Add the potato slices to the pan and cook for 1 minute so they get a light golden colour. Turn them over and place the monkfish fillets on top along with the artichokes, capers, parsley, garlic and wine. Cover with the slices of prosciutto. Transfer to the oven to roast for 6–8 minutes until the monkfish is cooked: it should feel firm but a bit springy in the middle.

5 Squeeze the lemon juice into the pan and add an extra dash of olive oil. Serve the monkfish and artichokes on the potatoes with the prosciutto on top and the pan juices spooned around.

12 Charlotte potatoes, peeled
1 large fennel bulb
2 tbsp extra virgin olive oil,
    plus extra for drizzling
2 whole red mullets, scaled and
    filleted (do this yourself or ask
    your fishmonger)
2 heaped tbsp pitted black olives,
    preferably Taggiasche
1 tbsp small capers in vinegar, drained
2 tbsp chopped parsley
200g Datterini or cherry tomatoes,
    cut in half
lemon juice
sea salt and freshly ground
    black pepper

This is a great way to cook red mullet because the fat from the fish melts into the potatoes and makes them taste delicious, as well as giving them a lovely colour and crisp texture. Serves 4.

roast red mullet fillet

with charlotte potatoes, fennel, olives and capers

1 Preheat the oven to 200°C. Cook the potatoes in a pan of boiling salted water for about 10 minutes until just tender; drain and cut into 5mm slices. While the potatoes are cooking, cut the fennel bulb lengthways in half, then cut each half into 1cm half-moon slices. Cook the fennel in another pan of boiling salted water for about 5 minutes until tender; drain.

2 Heat the olive oil in a large ovenproof frying pan and fry the potato slices until they start to colour. Add the fennel and fry for a minute longer.

3 Season the mullet fillets with salt and pepper, then place, skin side up, on top of the potatoes and fennel. Scatter the olives, capers, parsley and tomatoes over the fish. Transfer the pan to the oven and roast for 5 minutes.

4 Remove from the oven and finish with a squeeze of lemon and an extra drizzle of olive oil. Serve immediately.

20g dried porcini mushrooms
1 fennel bulb, thinly sliced
75g unsalted butter, plus extra
    for greasing
2 skinless pieces of organically
    farmed salmon fillet, about
    140g each
2 sprigs of thyme
50ml dry white vermouth
200g fresh spinach
extra virgin olive oil
sea salt and freshly ground
    black pepper

If you are lucky enough to get hold of some fresh porcini, this dish will be amazing. Fresh porcini are less concentrated than dried and will give a sweeter flavour. Dried porcini work really well too, but don't use too much or the flavour will be overpowering. Fennel with fish is always delicious. Serves 2.

salmon fillet
baked with fennel and porcini

1 Preheat the oven to 180°C. Put the porcini in a bowl of warm water and set aside to soak.

2 Meanwhile, blanch the fennel slices in a pan of boiling water for 2–3 minutes until just beginning to soften; drain. Butter a 60cm sheet of foil.

3 Place half of the fennel on one half of the buttered foil and arrange the salmon fillets on top. Season the salmon well. Drain the porcini and place half of them and a sprig of thyme on each fillet (if you are using fresh porcini, place them on top of the fish). Dot 25g butter over the fillets.

4 Fold over the foil and seal the edges to make a parcel, leaving one corner unsealed. Pour the vermouth through this gap, then seal the parcel completely. Set the parcel on a baking sheet and bake for 12 minutes.

5 While the fish is in the oven, bring a saucepan of water to the boil and add some salt, then place the spinach in the pan and cook for 1 minute. Drain in a colander and press out the excess water (do not run cold water on the spinach to refresh as this will dilute the taste). Season the spinach if required and add a dash of olive oil.

6 Remove the fish and vegetables from the foil parcel and arrange on plates with the spinach. Keep warm.

7 Pour the juice from the foil parcel into a saucepan and simmer on a medium heat until reduced by half. Whisk in the remaining 50g butter to thicken the sauce. Pour the sauce over the fish and serve.

8 fresh whole sardines
1 tbsp fennel seeds, crushed
grated zest and juice of 1 lemon
1 tbsp chopped parsley
1 dried red chilli
1 tbsp pine nuts
4 tbsp fresh breadcrumbs
extra virgin olive oil
sea salt and freshly ground
    black pepper

Although slightly time-consuming to prepare, this is an excellent way to enjoy a beautiful oily fish. The sardine fillets are layered with chilli, fennel seeds and breadcrumbs and then baked. The crumbs absorb some of the delicious sardine oils and become crisp. This is perfect with a simple salad of mixed tomatoes and basil dressed with olive oil. Serves 3.

sardino al forno

1 Scale the sardines and remove the gills. Slit open along the belly and remove the guts, then rinse well under cold running water until clean. Pat dry with kitchen paper.

2 Now fillet each fish. Starting at the tail end, use a sharp filleting knife to cut along both sides of the spine or backbone to the head. Use your fingers to work the flesh free of the spine between the tail and head. Cut off the tail and head to remove with the spine attached. This should leave the two fillets, without any of the tiny bones, attached by the skin where the spine was. Cut down the skin here to separate the fillets.

3 When you have finished filleting all the fish, preheat the oven to 180°C.

4 Lay four of the fillets, skin side down, side by side on a baking tray lined with greaseproof paper. Season with salt and pepper and sprinkle some of the fennel seeds, grated lemon zest, parsley, chilli, pine nuts and breadcrumbs over the fish. Make another two layers of sardine fillets, seasoning and sprinkling in the same way, then add a final layer of sardine fillets. Squeeze the lemon juice over the fish and add a drizzle of olive oil.

5 Bake for about 8 minutes. Serve hot.

2 tbsp extra virgin olive oil,
   plus extra for greasing
1 red onion, finely chopped
1 garlic clove, finely chopped
3 red peppers, seeded and
   cut into 2cm pieces
1 x 400g can chopped tomatoes
1 glass of red wine
small bunch of basil
6 fresh sardines, cleaned and gutted
   (do this yourself – see page 115 –
   or ask your fishmonger)
200g herb fennel sticks or
   50g herb fennel fronds
sea salt and freshly ground
   black pepper
lemon wedges, to serve

Sardines are usually great value for money and very good for you. Stuffing fennel sticks in the cavity of the fish flavours the sardine flesh perfectly. The best way to cook the fish is on a barbecue (don't put the sardines on the hottest part or they will flame due to their natural fish oils), but you can also use a ridged grill pan. Serves 2.

sardines grilled with fennel sticks,
with slow-cooked red peppers

1 Heat the olive oil in a heavy-based saucepan. Add the onion and garlic and cook for 5 minutes until softened. Stir in the red peppers and cook for 10 minutes. Add the tomatoes and red wine. Leave to cook gently for another 10 minutes, stirring occasionally, then season and add the roughly torn basil.

2 Meanwhile, heat a large ridged grill pan until it is very hot. Rub with a little olive oil on a clean cloth so the pan is clean and non-stick. Stuff each sardine with fennel sticks or fronds and season inside and out with salt. Place the fish in the hot pan and chargrill for about 2 minutes on each side until cooked through (you may need to cook a little longer, depending on size). Alternatively, cook the sardines on the barbecue.

3 Serve the sardines with lemon wedges, and with the slow-cooked peppers alongside.

200g ripe beef tomatoes
1 garlic clove, crushed to a paste
   with a pinch of flaked sea salt
5 basil leaves
150g ciabatta slices, toasted
5 tbsp extra virgin olive oil,
   plus extra for the fish
2 swordfish steaks, 2cm thick,
   about 200g each
1 tbsp chopped flat-leaf parsley
4 anchovy fillets (packed in oil),
   drained and finely chopped
1 tbsp small capers in vinegar, drained
sea salt and freshly ground black pepper

Swordfish when cooked rare can be very tasty, and served with this tomato and bread salad makes a perfect summer's day or holiday dish. Make sure you do not overcook the swordfish, or it will be dry and flavourless. Serves 2 generously.

seared swordfish
with pomodoro pugliese

1 Score the skin of the tomatoes, then put them in a pan of boiling water and leave to blanch for 1 minute. Remove the tomatoes with a slotted spoon and place in a bowl of cold water. When cool enough to handle, peel the skin off each tomato and cut out the tough core. Cut the tomatoes in half and chop to a fine dice.

2 Put the tomatoes in a bowl and add the garlic. Roughly tear up the basil and add to the bowl. Rip up the toasted ciabatta into 1cm pieces and add. Add the olive oil. Mix well so the ingredients are thoroughly combined. Season with salt and pepper to taste. Set aside.

3 Season the swordfish steaks and rub some olive oil on to both sides. Heat a frying pan until very hot, then add the swordfish steaks and cook for 1 minute. Turn the steaks over and add the parsley, anchovies and capers to the pan so they can fry in the fish juices and olive oil. After 1 minute, remove the steaks and place them on warmed serving plates. Pour the contents of the pan over the swordfish steaks so they are covered in parsley, anchovies and capers.

4 Serve the tomato and bread salad alongside the swordfish.

1 x 3kg whole turbot
50g small capers in vinegar, drained
2 tbsp chopped flat-leaf parsley
sea salt and freshly ground black pepper
squeeze of lemon juice, to serve

For the erbette
250g Swiss chard leaves,
    cut into quarters
250g curly kale
100g rocket
1 garlic clove, finely sliced
extra virgin olive oil, for frying
1 tsp fennel seeds, crushed
1 dried bird's eye chilli, crushed

Turbot is the best fish to roast on the bone as it has the most perfect combination of fat and natural gelatines. Searing on all sides before roasting is the way to cook individual portions. Make sure you rest the fish briefly before serving. The erbette is just a mixture of blanched greens, but tossed with really good olive oil and some fennel seeds and chilli makes it special. Serves 4.

turbot with erbette

1 Preheat the oven to 180°C. Start with the erbette. Blanch the Swiss chard leaves in a pan of boiling salted water for 3–4 minutes; lift out with a slotted spoon and drain. Blanch the kale in the same water for 5 minutes and drain, then blanch the rocket for 1 minute and drain. Lay all the greens flat on a tray and set aside to cool and dry while you prepare the fish.

2 Cut the wings off the turbot and remove the head. Cut down along the centre bone so you have two halves, then cut at right angles through the bone into four 180g steaks. Season the steaks with salt and pepper.

3 Heat an ovenproof frying pan until very hot. Add the turbot steaks, flesh-side down, and sear for 2 minutes. Turn the steaks over and sear for 2 minutes, then add the capers and parsley. Transfer the pan to the oven and roast for 10 minutes.

4 Meanwhile, finish the erbette. Fry the garlic in a little olive oil in a saucepan until just turning golden. Add the blanched greens, fennel seeds and chilli and toss in the hot oil for 2–3 minutes. Season. Squeeze the lemon juice into the pan with the turbot steaks, then leave to rest for 2 minutes before serving them with the erbette.

75g unsalted butter,
    plus extra for greasing
2 sea bass fillets (skin on),
    about 180g each
2 slices unwaxed lemon
4 basil leaves
100ml dry white vermouth
200g fresh spinach
extra virgin olive oil
sea salt and freshly ground
    black pepper

I love this dish because it is so simple. The juices in the parcels from the vermouth, lemon and basil mixed with the butter are so delicious with the sea bass. Spinach is just right with this dish but you could also add a few lentils. Serves 2.

sea bass
with lemon, vermouth and spinach

1 Preheat the oven to 190°C. Fold over two sheets of foil into large squares and butter the shiny sides.

2 Place a fish fillet, skin side up, on each buttered square of foil. Top each fillet with a slice of lemon, 2 basil leaves and 25g butter. Season with salt and pepper.

3 Fold the sides of the foil up around the fish and pour half of the vermouth into each pocket. Leave to settle for a few seconds, then crimp the foil edges together to seal.

4 Set the foil parcels on a baking tray and bake for 10–12 minutes. Check to see if the fish is cooked by carefully opening the parcels and piercing the fish with a sharp roasting fork: if it goes in with no resistance the fish is ready.

5 While the fish is in the oven, bring a saucepan of water to the boil and add some salt, then place the spinach in the pan and cook for 1 minute. Drain in a colander and squeeze or press out the excess water (do not refresh the spinach as this will dilute the taste). Season the spinach if required and add a dash of olive oil. Keep hot.

6 Once the fish is cooked, strain the juices from the parcels into a saucepan (set the fish aside in the foil to keep hot). Bring to the boil and reduce by half, then add the remaining butter.

7 Serve the sea bass topped with the butter sauce and with the spinach alongside.

2 stems herb fennel
2 gilthead bream, about 750g each,
   gutted and scaled by the fishmonger
extra virgin olive oil
150g Datterini tomatoes, cut in half
12 large green olives, such as
   Nocellara del Belice
1 tbsp caper berries
small bunch of parsley, chopped
1 garlic clove, sliced
sea salt and freshly ground
   black pepper

I always cook this dish when we go to Puglia on holiday. The first time I made it was after a family trip to Gallipoli. We'd bought a few bits and pieces from the beautiful shops and then I found myself outside this amazing fish market with the fattest, freshest sea bream looking at me. I HAD to buy it, using up my last 30 euros. The next two hours were somewhat fraught because my children had wanted ice creams and a drink. Not much was said in the car on the return from Gallipoli, apart from the occasional 'I'm thirsty'. When we got back, I quickly put the fish in the oven with some fennel tops underneath and a few tomatoes and caper berries on top. It came out of the oven all juicy, with the tomatoes and caper berries melted in with the juice. It was the best fish I have ever eaten, and everyone else reluctantly agreed it was worth sacrificing ice cream for. Serves 2.

roast bream
with tomatoes and caper berries

1 Preheat the oven to 180°C. Put a fennel stem in the stomach cavity of each bream, then season the fish inside and out with salt and pepper. Score a few slashes along both sides of the fish. Pour some olive oil into a roasting tin, then lay the fish in the tin.

2 Mix together the tomatoes, olives, caper berries, parsley and garlic with a drizzle of oil. Scatter over the fish. Roast the fish for 12–15 minutes until a skewer inserted into the thickest part meets with no resistance.

3 Remove the tin from the oven and leave the fish to rest in a warm place for a few minutes, before serving with blanched chard or another leafy green vegetable.

6 cleaned squid with tentacles
extra virgin olive oil
1 fresh red chilli, seeded and
   finely chopped
3 anchovy fillets (packed in oil),
   drained and chopped
2 tbsp chopped flat-leaf parsley
juice of ½ lemon

For the beans
2 plum tomatoes
1 x 400g jar or can cannellini beans,
   drained (rinse if canned)
sprig of sage
1 fresh red chilli, pricked with a knife
1 garlic clove, cut into quarters
3 tbsp extra virgin olive oil
1 tsp red wine vinegar
sea salt and freshly ground
   black pepper

To serve
250g wild rocket, chopped and
   dressed with olive oil and lemon juice

pan-fried squid
with beans, chilli, anchovy and rocket

I put this dish on the menu when we first opened the restaurant and due to its popularity it's still on. It's important to use squid that isn't too big – the body should be no longer than 20cm. Bigger than that and it will be too tough and should be braised instead. Also, make sure the pan is really hot before you put the squid in to cook. If you have time, make this with dried beans (cannellini or borlotti): soak them overnight, then simmer gently in three times their volume of water with the sage, chilli, garlic and tomatoes for about 1 hour until tender. Use about a quarter of the cooking liquor for the bean mix. Serves 4.

1 Start with the beans. Score the skin of the tomatoes, then put into a pan of boiling water and leave to blanch for 1 minute. Transfer to a bowl of cold water using a slotted spoon, then remove the skin. Chop the tomatoes. Put the beans in a saucepan with the tomatoes, sage, chilli, garlic and 100ml water. Simmer gently for 10–15 minutes.

2 Meanwhile, cut each squid body in half lengthways and open out flat, skinned side down. Score with a sharp knife in a criss-cross pattern. Set aside with the tentacles.

recipe continues overleaf

pan-fried squid with beans, chilli, anchovy and rocket *continued*

3 Discard the chilli and sage from the beans. Remove the garlic and mash it with a fork, then return to the beans. Season with salt and pepper and add the olive oil and vinegar. Stir to mix, then keep warm.

4 Season the squid with salt and pepper and rub a little olive oil into the scored flesh. Set a non-stick frying pan over a medium heat. When hot, add the squid pieces, scored side down, along with the tentacles. Cook for 1 minute until golden brown, then turn the pieces over. Add the chilli, anchovies, parsley and lemon juice to the pan.

5 Remove the squid and quickly slice into bite-size pieces. Return to the pan and toss briefly over the heat to mix with the other ingredients.

6 To serve, spoon the bean mixture into the centre of each plate. Place a small amount of rocket on top and then the squid.

juice of ½ lemon
3 violet artichokes with long stems
1 large aubergine
2 litres sunflower oil, for deep-frying
6 small courgettes with their
     flowers attached
2 cleaned squid (with tentacles),
     bodies cut into rings
8 large raw prawns,
     peeled but tails left on
4 sage leaves
sea salt and freshly ground
     black pepper

For the batter
300g tipo 00 flour
4 tbsp extra virgin olive oil
250ml warm water
1 organic egg white

To finish
1 fresh red chilli, chopped
2 sprigs of mint, chopped
lemon wedges

fritto misto
con calamari e gamberoni

Squid and prawns are a good combination, ideal for a fritto misto. The trick here is to fry them as light and crisp as possible, so always use clean sunflower oil and make sure you drain them well of any excess oil. Serves 2 as a main dish or 4 as a starter.

1 Fill a large bowl with water and add the lemon juice (or a handful of parsley stalks, which will do the same job), then prepare the artichokes one at a time. Remove the tough outer leaves to reveal the pale inner heart. Open the heart and, using a teaspoon, scoop out the hairy choke. Peel the stem to remove the tough outside, leaving the tender core. Slice the artichoke lengthways into quarters. Without delay, immerse in the lemon water solution to prevent them from turning brown.

2 Cut the aubergine lengthways in half, then cut across into 1cm-thick half-moon shapes.

3 Put a deep pan containing the sunflower oil on to heat to 180°C. Preheat a warm oven.

4 To make the batter, put the flour into a large mixing bowl and make a well in the middle. Pour the oil into the well, then mix the olive oil and flour together while slowly adding the warm water. Mix until the batter is smooth with the consistency of double cream.

5 When the oil is nearly up to temperature, in another bowl whisk the egg white to soft peaks, then carefully fold into the batter.

6 Fry the vegetables, squid and prawns separately in batches: dip into the batter and shake off any excess, then deep-fry in the hot oil until crisp and light brown all over. Fry the sage leaves last, just for a minute. As each batch is fried, drain on kitchen paper, then keep warm in the oven.

7 Serve hot, finished with chopped chilli and mint and lemon wedges.

100g Castelluccio lentils
1½ garlic cloves, the whole clove
   peeled and half clove sliced
extra virgin olive oil
500g Swiss chard leaves
1 tsp fennel seeds, crushed
12 cleaned scallops (shucked, with roe)
1 tsp small capers in vinegar, drained
1 fresh red chilli, finely chopped
12 sage leaves
1 lemon
sea salt and freshly ground
   black pepper

This dish is all about the quality of the ingredients so try to use fresh scallops in the shell – they are so much better than the ones you buy in tubs. They are easy to shuck (take out of their shells) and clean. Serves 2 as a main dish or 4 as a starter.

pan-fried scallops
with chilli, sage and lemon and swiss chard

1 Put the lentils in a pan with the whole garlic clove. Cover with water and bring to a simmer, then cook for 20–25 minutes until tender. Drain the lentils. Season and add a good dash of olive oil, then keep hot.

2 While the lentils are cooking, trim out the thick central rib from the Swiss chard leaves, then cut the leaves across in half. Blanch the leaves in a pan of boiling salted water for about 3 minutes until tender. Drain well, squeezing out excess water. Heat 1 tablespoon olive oil in the empty pan and fry the sliced garlic with the fennel seeds for 30 seconds. Add the Swiss chard and stir to combine. Season with salt and pepper. Remove from the heat and keep hot.

3 Heat a heavy-based frying pan. Toss the scallops in a bowl with salt, pepper and olive oil. When the pan is very hot, carefully place the scallops in the pan and cook for 1 minute on each side until golden brown. Add the capers, chilli, sage leaves and a squeeze of lemon. Serve hot, with the lentils and Swiss chard.

There is nothing like a really good beef sirlion steak cooked rare. Having it with some deep-fried jerusalem artichokes and butternut squash works really well as these vegetables are quite sweet and have a lovely texture when they are deep-fried. Don't cut the vegetables too thick or they will be less crispy. Serves 2.

2 thick sirloin or ribeye steaks,
    about 200g each
extra virgin olive oil
sea salt and freshly ground black pepper

For the chilli-parsley sauce
1 garlic clove, peeled
1 fresh red chilli, seeded and finely chopped
1 tbsp chopped flat-leaf parsley
1 tsp red wine vinegar

For the vegetables
sunflower oil, for deep-frying
6 jerusalem artichokes
½ ripe butternut squash, deseeded
500ml full-fat milk
300g tipo 00 flour

beef sirloin
with deep-fried jerusalem artichokes and butternut squash

1 First make the chilli-parsley sauce. Finely chop the garlic, then sprinkle with a small pinch of sea salt and crush the garlic to a paste. Mix this with the remaining sauce ingredients in a bowl. Set aside.

2 Put a deep pan of sunflower oil on to heat to 180°C (or use a deep-fat fryer). Peel the artichokes and squash, then cut into 5mm slices. Put them in a bowl and pour over the milk. Leave to soak while you sear the steaks.

3 Heat a ridged grill pan until very hot, and preheat a warm oven. Season the steaks with salt and pepper and rub olive oil on to both sides. Place on the hot grill pan and press down with a fork so the fat starts to melt. Chargrill for 2 minutes on each side until golden brown. Remove the steaks from the pan to a warm plate and set aside to rest while you fry the vegetables.

4 Put the flour into a large bowl. You'll need to fry the vegetables in batches so the pan of oil won't be crowded. Take some artichoke and squash slices out of the milk and drop into the flour, tossing to coat. Transfer to a sieve and shake off excess flour, then slip into the hot oil. Deep-fry for 2–3 minutes until golden brown all over and crisp. Remove with a slotted spoon and spread on kitchen paper to drain. Sprinkle with salt, then keep hot in the oven while you fry the rest of the vegetables.

5 Trim the fat from the steaks, then cut each into three slices at an angle. Place on warm plates, add the fried vegetables next to the steak and drizzle the chilli-parsley sauce over everything.

super quick   quick   a little more time   **1 hour**
                                                          leisurely but worth it

1kg Swiss chard
5–6 tbsp extra virgin olive oil
1 red onion, chopped
2 carrots, chopped
1 x 400g can chopped tomatoes
1 x 400g jar or can chickpeas,
    drained (rinse if canned)
2 fresh red chillies, finely chopped
handful of chopped parsley
2 tbsp lemon juice
2 veal chops, about 300g each
1 tsp chopped rosemary
sea salt and freshly ground
    black pepper

Veal chops are a classic Italian meat dish that can be wonderful or very disappointing. The important thing to do here is to brown the chops all over using olive oil and the fat of the veal, cooking the chops rare, then transfer them to the oven to cook very gently for a couple more minutes. This way you will get a lovely juice in the pan and the chops will be tender and succulent. With the spicy chickpeas and chard you have a really good combination of flavours and textures. Serves 2.

veal chops
with chickpeas and chard

1 Cut the stalks from the chard and chop them roughly. Blanch both the stalks and the leaves in a pan of boiling water with a dash of olive oil for about 4 minutes. Drain.

2 Heat 3 tablespoons olive oil in a heavy-based pan. Add the onion and carrots and cook gently for 15–20 minutes until tender. Stir in the canned tomatoes and chickpeas. Continue cooking for about 10 minutes until thick.

3 Preheat the oven to 180°C.

4 Add the Swiss chard to the chickpeas and stir to mix, then cook for another 10 minutes. Add the chillies, parsley, lemon juice and a generous splash of olive oil. Season with salt and pepper to taste.

5 While the chard and chickpeas are cooking, heat a heavy-based ovenproof frying pan. Season the veal chops with salt, pepper, olive oil and chopped rosemary, then place them in the hot pan. When they are lightly golden on one side, turn them over and colour the other side. Transfer the pan to the oven to finish cooking the chops for 3–4 minutes.

6 Remove the veal chops from the pan and rest on a plate for 2 minutes before serving with the hot chickpeas and chard.

4 pork chops, 2cm thick
2 tbsp chopped rosemary
juice of 1 lemon
2 tbsp extra virgin olive oil,
    plus extra for serving

For the potato and leek al forno
1kg waxy potatoes such as Roseval or
    Charlotte, peeled and cut into 2cm pieces
250g leeks, cut into 2cm pieces
1 garlic clove, sliced
50g anchovy fillets (packed in oil), drained
1 tbsp extra virgin olive oil
400ml double cream
40g dry breadcrumbs
sea salt and freshly ground black pepper

I love pork chops but they can be a bit dry sometimes. The best way to avoid this is by asking your butcher for the top end loin chops – these have a nice amount of fat around the eye of the meat (they are very much like a ribeye steak). Whenever you cook pork, always remember: fat is flavour. The potato and leek al forno is really tasty because it has anchovies and cream in it – perfect with the pork. Serves 4.

pork chops
with potato and leek al forno

1 Preheat the oven to 180°C. Parboil the potatoes in boiling salted water for 10 minutes until just tender; drain. At the same time, blanch the leeks in another pan of boiling water for 5 minutes until tender; drain well. Put the potatoes and leeks in a large bowl.

2 Heat a saucepan and briefly fry the garlic and anchovies in the olive oil, then add the cream and cook gently for 5 minutes, stirring occasionally. Add to the bowl and gently mix with the potatoes and leeks. Season with salt and pepper to taste.

3 Turn into a baking dish. Cover with foil and bake for 30 minutes. Remove the foil. Scatter the breadcrumbs over the surface, then continue baking for 5–10 minutes until browned on top.

4 While the potato and leek dish is baking, prepare the chops. Preheat the grill to medium-high. Trim excess fat from the chops. Mix together the rosemary, most of the lemon juice, the olive oil and some seasoning. Rub on to both sides of the chops.

5 Grill the chops for 3 minutes on each side. Remove from the heat and leave to rest for 1 minute, then sprinkle with the rest of the lemon juice and a dash of olive oil. Serve immediately, with the potato and leek al forno.

5 tbsp extra virgin olive oil
juice of 1 lemon
3 garlic cloves, crushed
1 tbsp chopped rosemary
1 rump of lamb, with fat on, about 500g
Salsa Verde (see page 220), to serve

For the roasted vegetables
1 ripe onion squash
6 jerusalem artichokes
3 carrots
25ml extra virgin olive oil
1 tsp chopped thyme
1 garlic clove, finely chopped
sea salt and freshly ground black pepper

Lamb rump is very under-rated –
when marinated it has a wonderful
flavour and is surprisingly tender. Salsa
verde is the perfect sauce for the lamb
as it cuts the fattiness and gives a lovely
fresh taste. Serve with a young Rosso
di Montalcino. Serves 2.

lamb rump
with salsa verde

1 Mix together the olive oil, lemon juice,
garlic and rosemary in a bowl. Add the
lamb rump and turn to coat with this
marinade, rubbing it in well. Set aside
to marinate for at least 30 minutes.

2 Meanwhile, prepare the vegetables.
Preheat the oven to 190°C. Peel the onion
squash, cut it in half and remove the seeds.
Cut the squash into 3cm wedges. Peel the
jerusalem artichokes and cut into quarters.
Cut the peeled carrots lengthways in half.

3 Bring a pot of salted water to the boil, add
all the vegetables and cook for 4–5 minutes
until tender. Drain, then tip into a bowl. Add
the olive oil, thyme and garlic and season with
salt and pepper. Toss so all the vegetable
pieces are coated with the seasoned oil.

4 Spread out the vegetables in an
ovenproof dish, cover with foil and roast
for about 20 minutes until tender. Remove
the foil and return to the oven to brown
the vegetables for 5 minutes.

5 While the vegetables are roasting,
cook the lamb. Pat it dry with kitchen
paper to remove any excess marinade,
then season the lamb with salt and pepper.
Heat an ovenproof frying pan and, when
very hot, sear the lamb rump on all sides.
Transfer to the oven to finish cooking for
4–5 minutes. Remove from the oven
and leave to rest for a couple of minutes.

6 Slice the lamb lengthways into four pieces.
Serve on the roasted vegetables, with a good
spoonful of salsa verde on top of the lamb.

2 sturdy sticks of rosemary, 20cm long
6 x 2cm cubes sourdough bread
6 slices pancetta
4 Tuscan sausages, each cut across
   into 4 pieces
4 plum tomatoes, each cut into quarters

For the lentil salad
250g cooked Puy or Castelluccio
   lentils (or vacuum-packed or
   drained French canned lentils)
small handful of dandelion leaves
½ large radicchio, leaves separated
1 tbsp coarsely chopped mint
1 tbsp balsamic vinegar
3 tbsp extra virgin olive oil
sea salt and freshly ground
   black pepper

For this recipe it is important that you use fat, well-seasoned Tuscan sausages, which are made with a combination of cured and fresh meat. You can get them from most Italian delis. The bread on the rosemary sticks goes really crispy from the sausage fat and tastes great. Serves 2.

spiedino of sausages
with dandelion lentil salad

1 Preheat the oven to 180°C. Remove the leaves from the rosemary sticks, except for the leafy top.

2 Wrap each cube of bread in a slice of pancetta. Thread the pieces of sausage, pancetta-wrapped bread and tomato quarters on to the rosemary sticks, alternating the ingredients and dividing them equally between the sticks.

3 Lay the rosemary skewers on an oven tray or in a shallow ovenproof dish and roast for 15 minutes.

4 Meanwhile, make the lentil salad. Combine the lentils, dandelion and radicchio leaves and mint in a salad bowl. Dress with the balsamic vinegar, olive oil and seasoning.

5 Serve the skewers hot with the lentil salad.

1 rack of lamb with 8 rib bones,
    French trimmed by the butcher
1 tbsp extra virgin olive oil
1 tbsp chopped rosemary

For the salsa verde
3 tbsp chopped parsley
1 tbsp chopped mint
1 tbsp chopped basil
1 tbsp small capers in vinegar,
    drained and chopped
1 anchovy fillet (packed in oil),
    drained and finely chopped
½ tbsp Dijon mustard
4 tbsp extra virgin olive oil
sea salt and freshly ground
    black pepper

Known as *scottadito* in Italian cookery, this is a brilliant way to speed up the cooking of lamb cutlets. Kids love them prepared like this because you can pick them up with your fingers (*scottadito* refers to burning your fingers in your rush to eat). Salsa verde is a lovely sauce to go with the cutlets. Serves 2.

beaten lamb cutlets
with salsa verde

1 To make the salsa verde, mix together all the chopped ingredients in a bowl, then add the mustard and olive oil. Check and adjust the seasoning. Set aside.

2 With a sharp knife, cut through the rack of lamb to separate it into eight cutlets. Place one on a chopping board and lay a sheet of clingfilm on top. Using the flat part of a heavy knife or cleaver, gently hit the meaty part so it flattens to half the original thickness and spreads to twice the width. Repeat this process to flatten all the cutlets.

3 Heat a ridged grill pan or heavy-based frying pan until it smokes. Brush both sides of the flattened cutlets with olive oil, then sprinkle with rosemary, salt and pepper. Place the cutlets carefully on the hot pan and cook for 1 minute on each side.

4 Lift the cutlets on to warmed plates and drizzle over the salsa verde. Serve hot.

2 globe artichokes
50g pancetta cubes
1 calf's kidney, about 250g,
    trimmed of fat and sinew
50g cooked Puy lentils
    (or vacuum-packed or drained
    French canned lentils)
4 sage leaves, chopped
2 tbsp Marsala wine
2 tbsp crème fraîche
sea salt and freshly ground
    black pepper

I love calf's kidneys cooked like this because you get a lovely juice from them that works really nicely with the lentils and artichokes. Use a dry Marsala – a sweet one will be too overpowering. Serves 2.

calf's kidneys
with pancetta, artichokes and marsala

1 Cook the artichokes whole in a covered pan of boiling salted water for about 15 minutes until tender. Check they are cooked with a sharp knife: it should go through the stem without any resistance. Drain.

2 When the artichokes are cool, peel off the outer leaves and peel the stem. Cut off the tough pointed top and scoop out the hairy choke. Cut each artichoke lengthways into eighths and set to one side.

3 Heat a heavy-based frying pan until very hot. Add the pancetta and cook until crisp. Use a slotted spoon to remove the pancetta, leaving the fat in the pan. Set the pancetta aside.

4 Break the kidney into lobes and season with salt and pepper, then add to the pan. Fry for about 2 minutes, turning the pieces over when they have a light brown colour. Add the lentils, chopped sage and artichokes, and mix with the kidneys.

5 Add the Marsala wine and boil to reduce the liquid by half. Stir in the crème fraîche and the crisp pancetta. Serve hot, with creamy mashed potato.

500g fresh spinach (stalks on)
3 tbsp extra virgin olive oil
½ garlic clove, sliced
1 x 400g jar or can cannellini
    beans, drained (rinse if canned)
8 slices smoked pancetta
8 sage leaves
50g unsalted butter
4 large slices calf's liver, 1cm thick
4 tbsp balsamic vinegar
4 tbsp crème fraîche
sea salt and freshly ground
    black pepper

Calf's liver is probably the easiest type of offal to cook. I like it when it is not too thinly sliced so you can get some colour on both sides when you cook it in butter. It tastes best when it is medium-rare. Frying the pancetta in a dry pan so the fat melts makes the pancetta really crispy, perfect with the liver. Serves 4.

pan-fried calf's liver
with cannellini beans, spinach, pancetta and sage

1 Blanch the spinach in a large pan of boiling salted water just until wilted and tender. Drain well, then season and toss with 2 tablespoons olive oil. Keep warm.

2 Heat the remaining olive oil in a small pan and briefly fry the garlic. Add the cannellini beans and cook for 2–3 minutes. Season and set aside in a warm place.

3 Heat a large frying pan, add the pancetta and cook until crisp. Remove with tongs and place on kitchen paper to drain. Add the sage leaves to the fat remaining in the pan and cook until crisp. Remove and set on top of the pancetta.

4 Wipe out the pan with kitchen paper, then add the butter. Heat until it foams, then carefully place the slices of calf's liver in the pan. Cook on a high heat for 2 minutes on each side.

5 Lift out the liver and place on warm plates. Add the spinach and a generous spoonful of cannellini beans next to the liver, then set the pancetta and sage on top. Pour the balsamic vinegar into the frying pan and boil to reduce by half, then stir in the crème fraîche. Spoon this sauce over the liver and serve.

2 fennel bulbs
300g Charlotte potatoes,
    peeled and cut into 5mm slices
5 garlic cloves (in their skin)
3 tbsp extra virgin olive oil
2 large chicken legs
1 tbsp picked thyme leaves
100g Datterini or cherry
    tomatoes, cut in half
sea salt and freshly ground
    black pepper

The legs are the best part of a chicken – they have lots of flavour because they are the part that does the most work. The crisp skin on the leg is the best bit. When they are cooked this way they produce a lovely juice that is absorbed into the potatoes and fennel. My wife Natalie cooks the best chicken I know, so the inspiration for this dish comes from her and her mother Josselyn. Serves 2.

roast chicken legs
with potatoes, fennel, tomatoes, thyme and garlic

1 Preheat the oven to 180°C. Trim the fennel bulbs. Cut each lengthways in half and then into 8 wedges. Cook the fennel in a pan of boiling salted water for about 5 minutes until tender. Use a slotted spoon to take the fennel out of the pan and put to one side in a bowl. Keep the water in the pan boiling.

2 Add the sliced potatoes and unpeeled garlic cloves to the boiling water and cook for about 8 minutes until tender. Drain and add to the bowl.

3 Heat a shallow flameproof casserole or ovenproof frying pan and add 1 tablespoon olive oil. Season the chicken legs with salt and pepper, then place them, skin side down, in the pan. Cook for about 2 minutes until there is a little colour on the skin. Turn the chicken legs over and cook for another 2 minutes. Remove from the heat and take the chicken legs out of the pan.

4 Add the thyme and tomatoes to the fennel, garlic and potatoes with the remaining olive oil and salt and pepper to taste. Tip the mixture into the hot casserole or frying pan and spread out evenly, then leave on a low heat for about 5 minutes so the potatoes start to go slightly crispy.

5 Place the chicken legs on top of the potato mixture. Add 2 tablespoons water to the pan, then transfer to the oven and cook for about 20 minutes until the chicken is thoroughly cooked. Serve hot, in the cooking pan.

1 pheasant, about 1kg
1 stem of rosemary
4 slices pancetta
1 small celeriac, peeled
    and cut into 1cm pieces
2 tbsp extra virgin olive oil
2 tbsp dry Marsala wine
300ml milk
50ml double cream
1 garlic clove, sliced
sea salt and freshly ground
    black pepper

Pheasant is a very difficult bird to get right as it tends to be easily overcooked and dry. The meat is very dense so simply roasting it whole isn't very successful – the breast is perfect slightly rare but the legs need much more cooking. Simmering it in milk and cream with celeriac brings out its flavour really well and keeps it tender. You also end up with the most amazing sauce. Serves 2.

pheasant
cooked in milk with celeriac

1 Preheat the oven to 180°C. Stuff the pheasant with the rosemary and season with salt and pepper, inside and out. Wrap the pancetta slices over the pheasant to protect the breasts and tie string around the bird so that the pancetta is secure and will not fall off. Set aside.

2 Cook the celeriac in a pan of boiling salted water for about 10 minutes until a knife will go through the pieces easily. Drain and put to one side.

3 Heat a heavy-based ovenproof pan, add the olive oil and sear the pheasant to give it a light golden colour all over. Take the pheasant out of the pan and discard the fat. Add the Marsala wine and boil to reduce for 1 minute. Add the cooked celeriac, milk, cream and garlic and bring to the boil. Remove from the heat.

4 Put the pheasant back in the pan and cover with greaseproof paper so the paper sits on top of the pheasant. Cook in the oven for 12–15 minutes until the juices run clear when the pheasant thigh are pricked with a skewer. Remove the greaseproof paper and return the pan to the oven to cook for a further 5 minutes, so that the juice can reduce and the pheasant can get a little more colour.

5 Transfer the pheasant to a chopping board and leave to rest for 10 minutes (keep the celeriac warm). Remove the string and, using a sharp knife, cut along the breastbone to take off the breasts. Then cut off the legs.

6 Place the breasts and legs on a warm plate and spoon over the celeriac and creamy cooking juices. Serve with some simple steamed spring greens tossed with good olive oil.

1 guinea fowl
150g mascarpone
leaves from 4 sprigs of thyme, chopped
grated zest and juice of 1 lemon
4 slices prosciutto di Parma
1 tbsp extra virgin olive oil
2 slices of sourdough or pagnotta bread
sea salt and freshly ground black pepper

For the salad
1 head of castelfranco, leaves
    separated and roughly torn
4 tbsp extra virgin olive oil
juice of ½ lemon
250g drained cannellini beans
    from a jar or can (rinse if canned)

To finish
chopped mint
balsamic vinegar

boned guinea fowl
stuffed with prosciutto, mascarpone and thyme with castelfranco salad

Guinea fowl is very under-rated. I love it, particularly prepared this way. Do use a good Altamura semolina-based bread or a good sourdough that is dense enough to absorb the fat from the bird – the bread will go crispy on the bottom while the juices from the guinea fowl will soften the top. It is delicious, perfect with the guinea fowl, cannellini beans and castelfranco (if you cannot get castelfranco you can use radicchio). The addition of fresh mint brings all the flavours together. In winter, I would serve the guinea fowl with some braised portobello mushrooms and greens. Serves 2.

1 Bone out the guinea fowl, leaving the wing bones intact: lay the bird breast down and use a sharp knife to cut through the skin along both sides of the backbone, then carefully ease the knife into the cuts and down around the carcass on both sides to separate it from the flesh; take care not to cut through the skin. Cut through the leg and wing joints, then remove the rib cage and backbone. Now cut the boned bird in half so you end up with two pieces each comprising a breast, leg and wing.

2 Next bone the legs. Insert a sharp knife into the flesh, to the bone, then cut down one side of the bone and around it to free it from the flesh.

recipe continues overleaf

boned guinea fowl stuffed with prosciutto *continued*

3 Preheat the oven to 200°C. Mix together the mascarpone, thyme, lemon zest and juice, and some seasoning.

4 Lay one of the boned guinea fowl halves, skin side down, on a chopping board. Pull the breast meat back to expose a cavity. Roll a spoonful of the mascarpone mix in a slice of prosciutto, then put it into this cavity. Fold the breast fillet back down over the filling so that it is enclosed between the skin and the breast. Repeat the same process to stuff the leg. Stuff the other guinea fowl half in the same way.

5 Heat a heavy-based ovenproof frying pan until hot and add the olive oil. Season the guinea fowl halves and place, skin side down, in the pan. Cook for 2 minutes until the skin is golden.

6 Drain off any excess fat from the pan, then tuck a slice of bread under each piece of guinea fowl. Transfer the pan to the oven and cook for 10–12 minutes. Remove from the oven and leave to rest for 4 minutes.

7 Meanwhile, for the salad toss the castelfranco with 2 tablespoons olive oil, the lemon juice, and salt and pepper to taste. In another bowl, mix the cannellini beans with the remaining olive oil and seasoning to taste.

8 Put a slice of the baked bread into each pasta bowl. Scatter the castelfranco and cannellini beans over the bread, then place the guinea fowl on top. Finish with chopped mint and a drizzle of balsamic vinegar.

4 squab pigeons
1 glass of Marsala wine
2 garlic cloves, sliced
a few sprigs of thyme
extra virgin olive oil
4 slices of pagnotta
   or sourdough bread
8 slices pancetta
150g fresh porcini mushrooms
   (or portobellos), sliced
500g Swiss chard
sea salt and freshly ground
   black pepper

boned squab pigeon

marinated in marsala and roasted on bruschetta, with chard and porcini

Squab pigeons are rather special and very different from wood pigeons as they are reared and not wild. (Wood pigeon has a lot of flavour, but it is better slow-cooked, otherwise it will be tough.) Marsala wine is great with the squab pigeon as it brings a sweetness to the slight gaminess of the bird. Serves 4.

1 First bone out each pigeon: use a small sharp knife to cut through the skin down both sides of the backbone. Get the knife under the skin and work around the carcass to ease the flesh from the bones; ensure you don't cut through or rip the skin as you go. Bone the whole bird except the legs.

2 Put the pigeons in a bowl and add the Marsala wine, half the garlic and the thyme. Leave to marinate for 1 hour.

3 Preheat the oven to 180°C. Heat a little olive oil in a large heavy-based ovenproof frying pan and sear the pigeons for 1 minute on each side (reserve the pigeon marinade). Turn them skin side down. Add the bread and pancetta to the pan, then transfer it to the oven to roast for 4 minutes.

recipe continues overleaf

boned squab pigeon marinated in marsala *continued*

4 Remove from the oven and place the pigeons, skin side up, on the bread. Return to the oven and roast for a further 3 minutes. When the pigeons are cooked, transfer to a chopping board (with the bread and pancetta), cover with foil and leave to rest. Reserve the cooking juices in the pan.

5 While the pigeons are roasting, heat a splash of olive oil in another frying pan, add the remaining garlic and cook briefly to soften. Add the porcini and fry for 3–4 minutes. Set aside in a warm place.

6 Remove and discard the chard stalks; cut the leaves into quarters. Blanch the chard leaves in a pan of boiling salted water for 5 minutes until tender. Drain well, then dress with some olive oil and seasoning. Keep hot.

7 Pour the reserved marinade into the ovenproof frying pan and boil to reduce by half, to make a little sauce; check the seasoning. Meanwhile, cut each pigeon into two pieces at an angle so you have two legs on one half and the breast on the other.

8 Place a slice of bread on each plate and spoon the porcini on to the bread. Set the pieces of pigeon on top and add the chard and pancetta. Drizzle over the Marsala sauce.

4 grey partridges
4 sprigs of thyme
12 slices pancetta
2 tbsp extra virgin olive oil
1 glass of port
1 Savoy cabbage, cored and shredded
1 garlic clove, sliced
1 tbsp finely chopped carrot
1 tbsp finely chopped onion
1 tbsp finely chopped celery
150g vacuum-packed peeled
   cooked chestnuts, roughly chopped
500ml chicken stock
sea salt and freshly ground
   black pepper

Grey partridge is the King of partridges. It is often referred to as a grey-legged partridge, which is wrong but understandable because of the popularity of its cousin, the red-legged partridge. There is no comparison though as the red-legged partridge tends to be farmed and lacks gaminess. Savoy cabbage is the natural partner for partridge. The more you cook it, the better it tastes as the natural sugars in the cabbage caramelises and becomes sweet. Use the darkest green outer leaves as they have the most flavour. Serves 4.

roast grey partridge
with savoy cabbage and pancetta

1 Preheat the oven to 180°C. Stuff a thyme sprig into each partridge, then wrap 3 slices of pancetta around each one and tie in place. Heat 1 tablespoon olive oil in a large heavy-based ovenproof pan and sear the partridges until lightly golden all over.

2 Turn the partridges breast down and transfer the pan to the oven to roast for 6 minutes. Turn the birds over and add the port to the pan, then roast for a further 5–6 minutes until the partridges are done: pull a leg away slightly from the breast to see if the meat looks cooked. When the birds are ready, remove from the oven and set aside to rest for 5 minutes. Remove the string.

3 While the partridges are roasting, blanch the Savoy cabbage in a pan of boiling salted water for about 7 minutes until tender; drain well. Heat the remaining olive oil in the empty pan and briefly fry the garlic. Add the chopped vegetables and chestnuts and cook for 4–5 minutes until softened. Add the cabbage and stock. Bring to a simmer, then cook on a low heat, stirring frequently, for 10–15 minutes until the stock has reduced and the cabbage becomes slightly caramelised. Season with salt and pepper.

4 Spoon the cabbage on to warmed plates, set the partridges on top and drizzle over the roasting juices.

main dishes
for feasts

These are the dishes for more leisurely
lunches and suppers, when you have
a bit more time to spend in the kitchen
and you want to cook something special
for friends and family. They're impressive
dishes but – like my other recipes in this
book – uncomplicated. One of my favourite
recipes here is the fish stew. It's a great
mixture of seafood with different flavours
and textures in a delicious saffron-tomato
broth. This is the kind of dish you can serve
in a huge bowl and dish up at the table.
The whole effect of bringing in the fish
stew from the kitchen is so impressive.
It may get a bit messy when you serve
it but that doesn't matter because you
have presented it so beautifully.

feasts

I remember having an amazing meal in Le Marche with David Gleave, Rose Gray and many others. We were guests of a local wine cooperative and they were out to impress 'Signor Gleave' (David is a very successful Master of Wine and imports the best wines from Italy for his company Liberty Wines). We sat at parallel tables facing the winemakers who were no doubt wondering who we were. The antipasti arrived, an amazing selection of fish carpaccio, prawns, raw langoustines and lobster. This was served with a basket of simple bread and a really fruity olive oil. I was in heaven and proceeded to have seconds and thirds.

Then the pasta courses started to arrive. Firstly there was tagliarini with cherry tomatoes, parsley, garlic and sweet lobster. This was followed by paccheri with vongole, white wine, prawns and parsley. And then there was another tagliarini with langoustine and zucchini. I wanted to try each of them again – so I did.

Next came a perfect fish risotto. My eyes and stomach were not in coordination so I had to have another helping. (I was not the only one eating like this. We were all blown away by the quality of the food.) Then came the little fish: first a large plate of little soles roasted to perfection in olive oil, garlic and parsley, and then little wild gilthead bream (one of my favourites) again roasted but with caper berries, tomatoes, parsley and white wine.

At this point there was a lot of belt loosening and a few whispers wondering how many more courses to go. We had all had way too much to eat. But the winemakers kept pouring the wine and kept on eating. In this situation the only thing you can do is to carry on, otherwise it looks rude.

All of a sudden the lights went out and we could just make out a trolley being pushed in by two chefs with huge toques on. They lit sparklers on what looked like a huge long cake. We all yelped with delight as this must be the end of the meal.

But no. When the sparklers went out and the lights came back on, sitting in the middle of this trolley was an enormous grouper fish staring at us with an orange in its mouth and its belly stuffed with potatoes, pancetta and parsley.

I don't think any of us ate the next day. That was the feast of all feasts.

20g dried porcini mushrooms
500g sea bass fillets
200g monkfish fillet
200g John Dory fillets
1 cooked lobster, about 500g
300g fresh clams (palourde) in shells
2 tbsp extra virgin olive oil
1 small onion, finely chopped
1 celery stick, finely chopped
2 small carrots, finely chopped
1 large fennel bulb, finely chopped
2¼ garlic cloves, 2 of them sliced
    and ¼ clove finely chopped

1 tsp fennel seeds, crushed
2 x 400g cans chopped tomatoes
    or 700ml tomato passata
500ml fresh fish stock (for home-made,
    see recipe on page 220)
200g potatoes such as Roseval, peeled
pinch of saffron threads
100ml white wine
leaves from a small bunch of parsley,
    finely chopped
sea salt and freshly ground
    black pepper

fish stew

I love making this dish. Once you have prepared the fish stew base, the rest is easy. Just make sure the base (the tomato-fish broth) is not too thick, otherwise the fish will cook unevenly. The lobster is essential because of the flavour it adds. The stew is finished with chopped garlic and fresh parsley at the end. Serves 4.

1 Put the porcini in a bowl with 100ml hot water and leave to soak until softened; drain the mushrooms (reserve the soaking liquid) and roughly chop.

2 While the porcini are soaking, prepare the seafood. Cut all the fish fillets into 3cm pieces. Remove the head from the lobster and pull off the claws; crack the claws. Cut the tail lengthways in half and then across in half. Put the clams in a colander and rinse thoroughly under cold running water, shaking the colander vigorously; discard any clams that remain open. Set the seafood aside in a cool place.

3 Heat 1 tablespoon olive oil in a large pan and cook the onion, celery, carrots and fennel bulb with the sliced garlic and fennel seeds until softened. Add the chopped porcini with their soaking liquid (leave any sediment behind in the bowl) and the tomatoes or passata. Cook for about 20 minutes to reduce by half, stirring occasionally. Add the fish stock and cook for another 20 minutes.

4 Meanwhile, cut the potatoes into thumb-size pieces. Put them in a pan of salted water with the saffron and bring to the boil; drain and reserve.

5 Remove the tomato-fish broth from the heat. Taste and season with salt and pepper. Purée in the pan with a hand blender (or blitz in a food processor). Keep hot.

6 Heat the remaining olive oil in a large shallow pan with a tight-fitting lid. Add the fish and clams along with the white wine. Cover and cook for 1 minute. Jiggle the pan to help open the clams (if any are not open after 1 minute, throw them away). Add the smooth tomato-fish broth and saffron potatoes. Cover with the lid again and bring to the boil, then add the quartered lobster tail and claws. Simmer for a few minutes.

7 Mix together the parsley and finely chopped garlic. Stir into the stew and heat, covered, for 1 minute. Serve in large bowls.

3kg rock salt
small bunch of basil
1 x 4kg organically farmed salmon,
   gutted (skin and fins left intact)
aïoli, preferably home-made
   (see recipe on page 221), to serve

For the grilled vegetables
2 aubergines
5 courgettes
2 red peppers
200g Datterini or cherry tomatoes
4 tbsp extra virgin olive oil,
   plus extra for drizzling
small bunch of basil
½ tbsp red wine vinegar
sea salt and freshly ground
   black pepper

salmon baked in sea salt
with grilled vegetables

This is probably the nicest way to eat a farmed salmon. The salt acts like a little oven but also seasons the fish perfectly. The grilled vegetables are just right to serve with the fish because they are light and a perfect balance for the rich salmon flesh. Serves 6.

1 Preheat the oven to 180°C. Mix the salt with 150ml water in a large bowl to make a salty sludge. Spread a nice flat bed of this salty sludge in a large roasting tray. Put the basil into the cavity in the salmon and add a sprinkle of salt. Lay the salmon on the salt bed and cover with the remaining salty sludge so you form a salt pack that covers the salmon evenly and completely. Bake for 1 hour.

2 Meanwhile, start preparing the vegetables. Heat a ridged grill pan. Cut the aubergines into 1cm slices. Place on the hot grill pan in one layer and cook on a high heat for 3–4 minutes on each side until soft on the edges and marked with charred lines. Remove from the heat and leave to cool.

recipe continues overleaf

salmon baked in sea salt with grilled vegetables *continued*

3 Slice the courgettes lengthways on a mandoline to make very thin slices (about 3mm). Place in the grill pan in one layer and cook for about 1 minute on each side, turning once, until they have nice charred marks on them. Remove and leave to cool.

4 Char the red peppers in the grill pan until their skins are black all over. Put them in a bowl, cover with clingfilm and leave to cool for 10 minutes before scraping off the charred skin with a serrated knife. Cut the peppers in half and scrape out all the seeds. Rip the peppers into 2cm pieces and leave to one side.

5 Cut the tomatoes in half and toss with a good drizzle of olive oil, some salt and pepper and some torn leaves of basil in an ovenproof dish. Cook in the oven for 5 minutes. Leave to cool.

6 Remove the salmon from the oven and set aside for at least 30 minutes. During this time, the residual heat in the salt crust will cook the salmon evenly so it ends up pink and juicy.

7 In a bowl, mix the 4 tablespoons olive oil with the vinegar, a pinch of salt and some black pepper. Add the grilled vegetables and mix together, then fold in the cooked tomatoes and some torn basil leaves. Check the seasoning.

8 Using a bread knife, carefully cut around the salt crust so that it comes off in big chunks and exposes the fish. With a sharp little knife, cut up from the tail so that the skin comes off in one piece (this way you do not lose any of the juices). Serve the salmon warm with the grilled vegetables (at room temperature) and aïoli.

120g sliced coppa di Parma
1 boned pork loin joint, about 1kg,
　　without rind and excess fat
　　(not rolled and tied)
30g unsalted butter, softened
leaves from 1 sprig of rosemary, chopped
grated zest and juice of 1 lemon
extra virgin olive oil
1 glass of sweet wine such as
　　Recioto di Soave
Salsa d'Erbe (see recipe
　　on page 219), to serve

This dish looks very impressive when it comes out of the oven. The coppa di Parma goes crispy as the fat melts into the pork and seasons the meat beautifully. Pork slightly pink is what you should aim for, and the sauce made in the roasting tin should be dark and slightly sweet. Pork should always be well rested after cooking – it is a very dense meat and will hold the heat well. If cut when hot it will lose its juices and be dry. Serve this with Potato, Parmesan and Fennel al Forno (see page 193). Serves 4.

pork loin
wrapped in coppa di parma

1 Preheat the oven to 180°C. Arrange the slices of coppa on a large sheet of greaseproof paper so they slightly overlap and make a shape big enough to wrap around the pork loin. Lay the pork out flat, skinned side down, on the coppa.

2 Mix the butter with the rosemary and lemon zest and juice to make a paste. Spread this evenly over the pork loin. Roll up the pork in the coppa, using the paper to help you roll, and tie up with string. (Keep the sheet of paper.)

3 Heat a heavy roasting tin on the hob and add a splash of olive oil. Place the pork loin in the tin and sear on one side for 2 minutes. Turn over and put the greaseproof paper on top. Transfer to the oven to roast for 30–40 minutes until a fork or skewer will go easily into the centre (an instant-read thermometer should register an internal temperature of 60°C).

4 Remove the pork loin from the tin and set aside to rest. Meanwhile, deglaze the tin with the sweet wine and cook for 5 minutes until reduced. Put the pork loin back in the tin and baste over the heat for at least 2 minutes before removing the string and carving the meat. Serve with salsa d'erbe.

70g dried porcini mushrooms
2kg chuck steak, cut into 2cm cubes
3 tbsp extra virgin olive oil
5 celery sticks, finely chopped
1 garlic clove, sliced
3 small red onions, finely chopped
1 tbsp chopped rosemary
2 x 400g cans chopped plum tomatoes
375ml Chianti Classico
sea salt and freshly ground black pepper

I think beef and porcini are made for each other. This stew takes time to cook but the initial preparation is very easy. Once it is in the oven you can just leave it there until it is done. If you don't want to serve it right away, set it on the side in a warm place – this will allow the flavours to come out even more fully. Serves 8.

beef and porcini stew
with rosemary and tomato

1 Preheat the oven to 180°C. Put the porcini in a small bowl, cover with 150ml boiling water and set aside to soak.

2 Season the beef well with salt and pepper. Heat a flameproof casserole, then add 2 tablespoons olive oil. When the oil is hot, add the beef (in batches) and sear on all sides. As each batch is browned, remove from the pan and set aside.

3 Add the remaining olive oil to the pan along with the celery, garlic, onions and rosemary. Cook for about 5 minutes until the vegetables are softened.

4 Remove the soaked mushrooms from their bowl with a slotted spoon and add to the pan. Strain the soaking liquid through a fine sieve (to ensure there is no grit) into the pan. Boil to reduce the liquid by half, then add the chopped tomatoes and wine. Bring to a simmer.

5 Return the beef to the casserole. Cover it with greaseproof paper and place in the oven to cook for 2 hours. After this time the stew should be thick and the meat so tender that it breaks up easily. Check the seasoning before serving hot, with Wet Polenta (see recipe on page 36).

50g dried porcini mushrooms
1 x 2kg boned veal loin joint
1 tbsp chopped rosemary
grated zest and juice of ½ lemon
70–100g unsalted butter, softened
1 garlic clove, crushed
extra virgin olive oil, for frying
175ml white wine
sea salt and freshly ground
    black pepper

veal loin
with porcini and white wine

This has to be the best dish to cook for a dinner party as it is luxurious, easy to make and very easy to serve. I cooked it many years ago for Marcella Hazan when she came to the River Café. When she came into the kitchen I had my copy of one of her books at hand and she willingly signed it, then turned to me with a very cheeky grin and said, 'That was the best veal dish outside my home.' It doesn't get better than that!

I would normally serve Wet Polenta (see recipe on page 36) with something like this but a really good mash made with Spunta or Cyprus potatoes would also work perfectly, plus steamed spinach dressed in really good olive oil. Serves 8.

1 Preheat the oven to 180°C. Put the porcini in a bowl, cover with 100ml of boiling water and leave to soak.

2 Trim the loin of veal, then open it out flat, skin side down, on the worktop. It should be roughly even in thickness all over, so make slashes in the meat and press open if necessary. Season with salt and pepper, then sprinkle with the rosemary.

3 Mix together the lemon zest and a little lemon juice with most of the butter and the garlic in a small bowl. Massage this flavoured butter into the veal.

4 Roll up the veal and tie with kitchen string to secure. Season the outside.

5 Heat some olive oil with the remaining butter in a heavy-based frying pan over a high heat. Brown the veal all over, then transfer it to a roasting tin. Pour any excess fat out of the frying pan.

6 Drain the porcini, reserving the liquid. Add the porcini and half their soaking liquid (leave any sediment behind in the bowl) to the frying pan and bubble for a few minutes. Add the white wine and bring to the boil, then boil for 1–2 minutes. Pour the contents of the pan over the veal in the roasting tin.

7 Cover the roasting tin loosely with foil and roast for 30 minutes until an instant-read thermometer registers an internal temperature of 65°C. Halfway through cooking baste the veal with the juices in the tin.

8 Transfer the veal to a carving board, cover with foil and leave to rest in a warm place for 10 minutes, basting now and again with a little of the cooking juices.

9 Meanwhile, if the cooking juices in the tin don't have a sauce-like consistency, tip them into a saucepan and simmer until reduced. Taste and adjust the seasoning as necessary.

10 Remove the string from the veal and carve into 1cm-thick slices. Spoon over the sauce and mushrooms and serve.

1 x 1kg piece of roast veal loin (or pork loin)
100ml mayonnaise, preferably home-made
 (see recipe on page 221)
1 x 150g can best-quality tuna fish
 packed in olive oil, drained
juice of 1 lemon
1 tsp small capers in vinegar, drained
1 tsp chopped parsley
3 anchovy fillets (packed in oil),
 drained and sliced lengthways
sea salt and freshly ground black pepper

To serve
wild rocket, dressed with lemon juice
 and extra virgin olive oil

This is a perfect sharing dish for Sunday lunch. Typically Piedmontese, it's a great way to make some cold roasted meat taste delicious by adding a fresh mayonnaise seasoned with anchovy, tuna and capers. Try it with some blanched green beans and rocket. If you don't have any leftover roast veal you can cook a boneless loin joint the night before: simply rub with olive oil and sea salt, then roast in a preheated 180°C oven for 30 minutes and cool. Serves 4.

vitello tonnato

1 Thinly slice the cold veal loin and arrange on a large plate.

2 Blitz together the mayonnaise, half the tuna fish and the lemon juice in a food processor until smooth. Season with salt and pepper. Spoon evenly over the veal slices.

3 Scatter the capers, chopped parsley, anchovies and remaining tuna, flaked, on top. Serve with some dressed wild rocket.

1 x 1.5kg boned lamb shoulder
   (not rolled and tied)
2 tbsp extra virgin olive oil,
   plus extra for dressing the broccoli
6 garlic cloves, peeled
8 anchovy fillets
   (packed in oil), drained
sprig of rosemary
50g pitted black olives,
   preferably Taggiasche
250ml white wine
500g purple sprouting broccoli,
   tough stems removed
sea salt and freshly ground
   black pepper

I always do this dish when we have lots of people over for the very reason it is so easy to prepare and serve. Put it in the oven a couple of hours before your guests arrive and it will be ready in good time – so tender you can serve it with a spoon. Purple sprouting broccoli, just blanched in boiling salted water and dressed with good olive oil, makes a great accompaniment.
Serves 6.

lamb shoulder
with purple sprouting broccoli

1 Preheat the oven to 180°C. Trim excess fat from the lamb shoulder. Heat a flameproof casserole and add the olive oil, then put in the shoulder and sear to brown it on all sides. Take it out of the pan and pour off the excess fat.

2 Add the garlic cloves, anchovies, rosemary, olives and white wine to the casserole and set the shoulder on top. Cover tightly with a lid or foil and place in the oven to cook for 1–1½ hours until the meat is very tender, basting occasionally. Cook uncovered for the last 10 minutes or so to lightly reduce the cooking juices by about half.

3 Towards the end of the lamb cooking time, cook the purple sprouting broccoli in a pan of boiling salted water until tender. Drain and dress with olive oil and seasoning to taste. Serve the shoulder of lamb with its cooking juices and the broccoli.

1 small leg of lamb, no more than 2kg,
   boned and butterflied (do this yourself
   or ask your butcher)
leaves from 2 sprigs of rosemary
3 garlic cloves, sliced
6 anchovy fillets (packed in oil),
   drained and halved
3 tbsp extra virgin olive oil
Salsa Verde (see recipe on page 220),
   made with 6 anchovy fillets, to serve

For the vegetables
400g carrots, cut in half lengthways
2 fennel bulbs, each cut into 8 wedges
1 small, ripe onion squash, peeled,
   seeded and cut into 8 wedges
250g waxy potatoes, peeled and cut in half
2 tbsp extra virgin olive oil
5–6 garlic cloves
1 tsp chopped thyme
sea salt and freshly ground black pepper

leg of lamb
with roasted root vegetables

Root vegetables have such a lovely sweet flavour if you part-cook them in boiling salted water, then toss them with olive oil, garlic, salt and thyme before roasting. If you spread them on flat sheets so they are not on top of each other, they will caramelise nicely. After roasting the lamb make sure you rest it. If you slice it before it is well rested you will lose all its juices, making the meat dry. Serves 5–6.

1 Start with the vegetables. Add all of them to a large pan of boiling salted water and bring back to the boil, then cook for 10 minutes. Add the whole garlic cloves to the water and cook for 2 minutes. Drain.

2 In a large bowl, mix together the olive oil and thyme. Add the part-cooked vegetables and garlic cloves, season well with salt and pepper, and toss to mix. Line a roasting tray with a piece of greaseproof paper, then spread the vegetables on top. Set aside.

recipe continues overleaf

leg of lamb with roasted root vegetables *continued*

3 Preheat the oven to 180°C. Trim excess fat from the lamb. Make 12 incisions in the meat using a sharp knife, then fill each with a little rosemary, sliced garlic and anchovy. Season well with salt and pepper.

4 Put the tray of vegetables in the oven and roast for 5 minutes.

5 Meanwhile, heat a heavy roasting tin on the hob, add the olive oil and sear the fat side of the butterflied leg of lamb for 2 minutes. Turn the lamb over to briefly brown the other side.

6 Transfer the tin to the oven, to join the tray of vegetables. Roast for 25 minutes until the vegetables are caramelised and the lamb is cooked – test with an instant-read thermometer: the internal temperature should be 60°C for medium-rare.

7 Remove the lamb from the oven and allow to rest for at least 5 minutes. Meanwhile, turn the oven down low to keep the vegetables warm.

8 Slice the lamb and serve with the vegetables and the salsa verde drizzled over.

There is nothing like good pizza. I find that the best ones tend to be the simplest, with not too many ingredients on top, and a good tomato passata as the base. When making a pizza it's important to be sure that it cooks from the bottom as well as on top. A hot pizza stone helps with this, or you can use a heated baking sheet. If you don't do this you will have uncooked dough with a soggy base. Makes 1 big pizza.

For the dough stage 1
30g tipo 00 flour
2 tsp dried yeast
60ml lukewarm water

For the dough stage 2
200g tipo 00 flour, plus extra for dusting
½ tsp salt
120ml lukewarm water
1 tbsp milk
2 tbsp extra virgin olive oil, plus extra
    for greasing
semolina, for the baking sheet

For the topping
200ml tomato passata
3 slices prosciutto di Parma, torn into strips
2 x 150g balls buffalo mozzarella, torn into pieces
150g Datterini or cherry tomatoes, cut in half
1 tbsp oregano leaves
75g pitted black olives, preferably Taggiasche
50ml extra virgin olive oil

pizza

1 For stage 1 of the dough, put the flour and yeast into a large bowl and mix in the water. Leave in a warm place (35–40°C) for 15–20 minutes until frothy.

2 Add all the ingredients for stage 2 and mix together to a dough using a wooden spoon and then your hands. Turn out on to a floured surface and knead for 10–15 minutes to develop the elasticity of the dough.

3 Shape the dough into a ball and rub with olive oil to prevent a crust from forming. Place in a clean bowl, cover the bowl with a towel and leave the dough to rise in a warm place for about 1 hour until doubled in size.

4 Knock back the dough, then let it rise again for a further 40 minutes.

5 When you are ready to make the pizza, preheat the oven to 250°C, and put a pizza stone or a large baking sheet in to heat. Turn the dough on to a lightly floured work surface and roll out into a rough rectangle or other shape that is about 2cm thick. Lift on to a large, semolina-dusted baking sheet.

6 For the topping, spread the passata evenly over the pizza base to within 1cm of the edge. Add the remaining topping ingredients, scattering them evenly, then drizzle the olive oil over all.

7 Slide the pizza on to the hot baking stone or baking sheet in the oven and bake for 5–7 minutes. Serve hot.

For the pastry
250g unsalted butter, chilled
250g plain flour
5 tbsp ice-cold water

For the topping
50ml extra virgin olive oil
2 red onions, finely sliced
1 garlic clove, chopped
leaves picked from a small
 bunch of thyme, chopped
1kg fresh spinach
200g ricotta cheese
leaves from a small bunch
 of flat-leaf parsley, chopped
200ml crème fraîche
2 organic egg yolks
50g Parmesan cheese, freshly grated
100g Parmesan cheese shavings
4 slices prosciutto di Parma,
 torn into pieces (optional)

I love making this as a 'standing-up starter' when people come over – it is so easy and you can make it in advance and reheat it. The pasta frollo is an incredibly light pastry that tastes great with the topping of spinach, Parmesan, ricotta and slow-cooked onions. You could also have this as a lunch dish with a crisp green salad. Serves 6.

torta di pasta frollo

1 To make the pastry, put the butter and flour in a food processor and pulse to a breadcrumb consistency. Add the iced water and pulse just until a dough is formed. Wrap in clingfilm and chill in the fridge for 30 minutes.

2 Preheat the oven to 180°C. Roll out the pastry on a baking sheet to a rectangular shape about 5mm thick. Prick all over with a fork, then bake for 10 minutes until crisp. Set aside to cool. Leave the oven on.

3 Start making the topping while the pastry base is baking. Heat the olive oil in a large heavy-based pan, add the onions with the garlic and thyme, and cook on a low heat for about 15 minutes until softened.

4 Meanwhile, blanch the spinach in a pan of boiling water until wilted. Drain and, when cool enough to handle, squeeze or press the spinach to remove excess water. Chop the spinach.

5 Spread the cooked onions evenly over the pastry. Top with the spinach, the broken-up ricotta and chopped parsley. In a bowl, mix the crème fraîche with the egg yolks and grated Parmesan and drizzle this mixture over the spinach and ricotta. Bake for about 15 minutes until the topping is a light golden colour.

6 Scatter the Parmesan shavings over the pasta frollo and arrange the torn slices of prosciutto on top, if you like. Serve warm.

side dishes

Here is a selection of dishes to accompany
a main dish – often overlooked but important
to complement and round out a meal. Some
of them can also be served on their own,
as starters or even for a lunch or supper. For
example, roasted red peppers are delicious
with a whole roasted fish, but they're also
perfect as part of a selection of sharing
starters. And I think the baked spinach with
parmesan cream could be a meal in itself.
The potato and fennel al forno was inspired
by a dish I once made at Chez Panisse.
The sourdough crumbs on top of the
creamy potatoes go all crispy and it all
ends up slightly gooey on the edges.
Try it with my roast pork loin wrapped in
coppa di Parma – a perfect combination.

juice of ½ lemon
4 medium violet artichokes
   with long stems
500g Swiss chard
extra virgin olive oil
4 spring onions, finely chopped
200g shelled fresh peas
200g shelled fresh broad beans
2 tbsp chopped mint
sea salt and freshly ground
   black pepper

To serve (as a starter)
2 slices of ciabatta bread
1 garlic clove, cut in half
extra virgin olive oil

Looking through the recipes in this book you'll soon realise that globe artichokes are one of my favourite vegetables. This delicate spring/early summer dish combines them with other vegetables in season. If you are growing your own peas and broad beans, make sure you pick them when they are not too big, otherwise they won't be as sweet. When fresh peas aren't available, you can replace them with frozen, but I wouldn't recommend using frozen broad beans. Serves 4 as a side dish or 2 as a starter.

braised artichokes
with peas and broad beans

1 First fill a large bowl with water and add the lemon juice (or a handful of parsley stalks, which will do the same job), then prepare the artichokes one at a time. Remove the tough outer leaves to reveal the pale inner heart. Open the heart and, using a teaspoon, scoop out the hairy choke. Peel the stem to remove the tough outside, leaving just the tender core. Slice the artichoke lengthways into eight wedges. Without delay, immerse in the lemon water solution to prevent them from turning brown.

2 Cut the chard stalks from the leaves. Finely chop the stalks and roughly chop the leaves. Blanch the chard stalks in a pan of boiling water for 2–3 minutes; drain.

3 Heat a drizzle of olive oil in a small frying pan. Add the spring onions and cook for 2 minutes. Add the artichokes along with the peas, broad beans and finely chopped chard stalks. Pour in 100ml water. Cook for 10 minutes. Add the chard leaves and cook for a further 2 minutes.

4 While the vegetables are cooking, toast or grill the bread until golden brown on both sides. Rub with the garlic and brush with olive oil. Season with a little salt.

5 Stir the chopped mint into the vegetables. Cook for a further 1–2 minutes until the liquid has reduced to a thick, syrupy consistency. Season with salt and pepper and a drizzle of olive oil. Serve hot with the toasted ciabatta.

1.2kg fresh spinach (with stalks)
3 organic eggs
120g Parmesan cheese,
   freshly grated
250ml single cream
¼ nutmeg, freshly grated
extra virgin olive oil, for greasing
sea salt and freshly ground
   black pepper

This is a great recipe to make if all you have in the fridge are eggs, spinach and Parmesan and you don't fancy an omelette. It's important not to overcook the spinach when you blanch it, otherwise it may lose its fresh flavour when it's baked. Serves 4–6.

baked spinach
with parmesan, cream and nutmeg

1 Preheat the oven to 180°C. With this amount of spinach you'll need to blanch it in two batches. Add one batch (about half) to a large pot of boiling salted water and cook for 2 minutes. Use a slotted spoon to transfer the spinach to a colander set in the sink. (Do not refresh with cold water as this will dilute the flavour of the spinach.)

2 Cook the second batch in the same way and transfer to the colander. Using a spoon, press the spinach against the colander to remove excess water. With a pair of kitchen scissors, roughly cut up the spinach in the colander.

3 Beat the eggs, Parmesan and cream together in a large bowl. Add the spinach, nutmeg and seasoning.

4 Rub an earthenware or other baking dish with a little olive oil. Pour the spinach cream mixture into the dish and bake for 15 minutes until set. Serve hot.

1 tbsp raisins
750g fresh spinach (with stalks)
1 tbsp extra virgin olive oil
2 tbsp pine nuts, preferably Mediterranean
sea salt and freshly ground black pepper

I first had this in a trattoria in Rome and
it has always been a favourite at home.
It's a simple dish of spinach with sweet
raisins and pine nuts – delicious with
roast lamb or veal. Serves 2–3.

spinaci alla romana

1 Soak the raisins in hot water for
5 minutes; drain.

2 While the raisins are soaking, blanch
the spinach in a large pan of boiling salted
water for 1½–2 minutes until the stalks
are tender but still have a bite. Pour into
a colander and leave to drain – do not
refresh with cold water – then press
out the excess water.

3 Heat the olive oil in a large saucepan
or deep frying pan, add the pine nuts
and cook on a low heat until lightly
golden. Add the raisins and spinach
and toss well to mix and warm the
spinach. Season with salt and
pepper before serving.

**45 minutes, plus
rising and proving**
leisurely but worth it

900g strong white bread flour
100g semolina, plus extra for the tray
35g fresh yeast
pinch of caster sugar
15g sea salt
2 tbsp extra virgin olive oil,
    plus extra for greasing
500–550ml lukewarm water

To finish
extra virgin olive oil
flaked sea salt
chopped rosemary

We use this recipe in the restaurant, baking it in a convection oven with a little steam. The steam helps the focaccia rise. To get a similar effect at home, when you turn on your oven to preheat it, put a tray of hot water in the bottom. Be sure to use a good sea salt to sprinkle on top as this will make the focaccia really tasty. Makes 1 focaccia.

focaccia

1 Mix together the flour and semolina in a large bowl.

2 In another bowl, mix the yeast with the sugar. Add the salt, olive oil and 500ml lukewarm water and mix together.

3 Tip the yeast mixture into the flour and mix – by hand or in a food mixer fitted with the dough hook – to a soft but not sticky dough (you may need to add more water or flour).

4 Shape into a ball. Cover the bowl with clingfilm and leave the dough to rise in a warm place until doubled in size. During this time, oil a baking tray and sprinkle it with semolina.

5 Spread out the dough on the prepared tray to a rough rectangular or square shape about 2cm thick. Make indentations all over the dough with your fingertips. Sprinkle olive oil and flaked sea salt over the top and then some chopped rosemary. Leave to prove in a warm place for 10–15 minutes. Meanwhile, preheat the oven to 220°C.

6 Bake the focaccia for about 10 minutes until golden brown; it should sound hollow when tapped on the base. Drizzle more olive oil all over the top, then leave to cool on a wire rack before slicing or tearing into pieces.

4 red peppers
12 baby plum or cherry
    tomatoes, each cut in half
2 tbsp small capers
    in vinegar, drained
1 garlic clove, sliced
8 anchovy fillets
    (packed in oil), drained
8 basil leaves
50ml extra virgin olive oil
sea salt and freshly ground
    black pepper

The trick to this dish is to cook
the peppers slowly and gently so
that they end up beautifully sweet.
Serves 4 as a side dish or starter.

peperoni rossi arrostiti

1 Preheat the oven to 150°C. Cut the
peppers in half lengthways, keeping the
stems on if you like. Scoop out the cores,
ribs and seeds. Season the insides with
salt and pepper.

2 Arrange the pepper halves, cut side
up, on a wire rack set on a baking sheet.
Put 3 tomato halves, flat side down, into
each pepper half. Add capers, garlic, an
anchovy fillet, a basil leaf and a drizzle
of olive oil to each half.

3 Bake for 1 hour until the peppers are
soft all the way through but still moist –
looking almost like sun-dried tomatoes.
Serve warm.

1kg Roseval potatoes, peeled
   and cut into 2cm pieces
3 fennel bulbs, cut into
   2cm-thick wedges and
   fronds removed and finely
   chopped
250ml double cream
1 garlic clove, chopped
300g Parmesan cheese,
   freshly grated
100g breadcrumbs
sea salt and freshly ground
   black pepper

I first made this dish when I worked at Chez Panisse in Berkeley, California. It's important to use a good waxy potato – floury potatoes will become stodgy and break up. The combination of fennel, cream, potato and Parmesan is rich and delicious, perfect with a meat dish like Pork Loin Wrapped in Coppa di Parma (see recipe on page 165). Serves 4.

potato, parmesan and fennel al forno

1 Preheat the oven to 180°C. Cook the potatoes in a pan of boiling salted water for 10 minutes until just tender then drain.

2 At the same time, cook the fennel in another pan of boiling salted water for 3–4 minutes until tender. Drain.

3 Tip the potatoes and fennel wedges into a bowl and add the cream, garlic and Parmesan. Season with salt and pepper and stir to mix. Spoon into a baking dish, sprinkle with the chopped fennel fronds and breadcrumbs and then cover with foil.

4 Bake for 15 minutes. Remove the foil and bake for a further 5 minutes until the breadcrumbs are a light golden colour. Serve hot.

desserts

I like simple desserts and my favourites usually have fruit in them – for example, apricots with Amaretto and toasted almonds, which turns a scoop of vanilla ice cream into something amazing! And I love chocolate! Apparently the first word I ever said was chocolate so it's not surprising really. I find that the better the chocolate you use (preferably with 70 per cent cocoa solids), the better the dessert will taste. I also love desserts made with ricotta. In Sicily, ricotta is used in the same way as we use cream. I am a fan of cheesecakes as long as they aren't too rich, and I think my ricotta cheesecake is perfect (the addition of Marsala wine might have something to do with it!).

1 x 26cm Sweet Pastry Case
  (see recipe on page 221)

For the almond filling
300g blanched (skinned) almonds
300g unsalted butter, softened
300g caster sugar
3 organic eggs
crème fraîche, to serve

This tart makes a very versatile dessert because it can be served with all kinds of fruit. For example, in summer it is lovely with raspberries and crème fraîche or with baked fresh apricots (to bake apricots, cut them in half and remove the stones, then spread in a baking dish and sprinkle with vanilla sugar and Amaretto to taste; bake at 180°C until soft). Pears baked with lemon and sugar are good too. In winter try the tart with marinated prunes. It is always best freshly baked, when the pastry is crisp and the filling moist. Makes a 26cm tart

almond tart

1 Preheat the oven to 180°C. Line the tart case with baking parchment and fill with baking beans. Blind bake for 15 minutes until golden in colour. Remove the paper and baking beans, then return the tart case to the oven to bake for a further 5 minutes. Set aside. Leave the oven on.

2 Make the filling while the pastry case is baking. Grind the almonds in a blender or food processor; tip into a bowl and set aside. Cream the butter with the sugar in the processor until pale and fluffy. Add the almonds, then mix in the eggs one at a time until combined.

3 Spread the filling in the tart case. Bake for 30–40 minutes until the filling is golden brown. Cool before serving with crème fraîche.

1 x 26cm Sweet Pastry Case
   (see recipe on page 221)
beaten egg, for egg wash

For the filling
grated zest of 5 Amalfi lemons
150ml freshly squeezed Amalfi
   lemon juice
300g caster sugar
300g unsalted butter, chilled
6 whole organic eggs
9 organic egg yolks

The idea for this tart came from Lindsey Shere's brilliant book Chez Panisse Desserts. In the original recipe, the lemon curd filling is made with Meyer lemons, which are thought to be a cross between a mandarin and a lemon. They are abundant in Berkeley, California (where Chez Panisse is), growing in people's gardens there. I think the Amalfi, a beautiful large Italian lemon with a sweet taste and intense aroma, makes an excellent substitute. Makes a 26cm tart to serve 8.

amalfi lemon tart

1 Preheat the oven to 180°C. Line the tart case with baking parchment and fill with baking beans. Blind bake for 15 minutes until golden in colour. Remove the paper and baking beans, then return the tart case to the oven to bake for a further 5 minutes. Brush all over the inside of the case with egg wash to seal. Bake for another 5 minutes, then set aside.

2 Preheat the grill to high. For the filling, combine the lemon zest and juice, sugar and butter in a heavy-based saucepan and heat gently until the butter has melted and the sugar dissolved. Whisk the eggs and yolks together in a bowl, then add to the saucepan. Stir over a medium heat until the custard mixture thickens (make sure it doesn't boil or the eggs will curdle). Still stirring, pour the filling into the tart case.

3 Place the tart under the grill and cook until black patches appear on the surface of the filling. Leave to cool and set before serving.

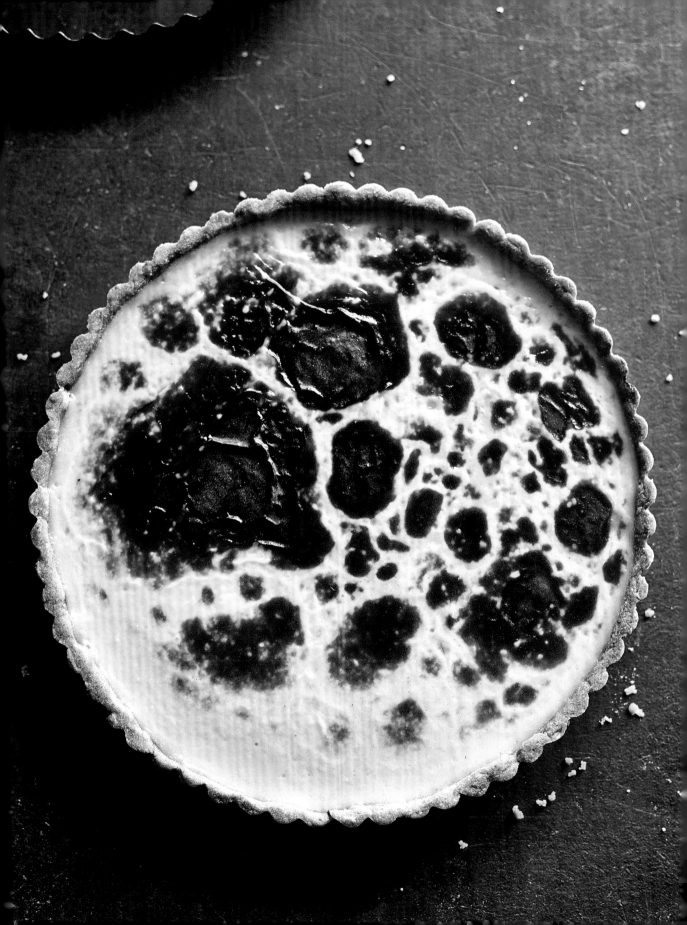

super quick quick a little more time **50 minutes, plus making pastry**
leisurely but worth it

1 x 26cm Sweet Pastry Case
  (see recipe on page 221)
beaten egg, for egg wash

For the filling
1 Earl Grey teabag
300g dried pitted prunes
4 tbsp Armagnac
3 organic eggs
110g caster sugar
seeds from 1 vanilla pod
grated zest and juice of
  4 clementines
5 tbsp double cream
4 tbsp chopped blanched
  (skinned) almonds
1 tbsp plain flour
icing sugar, for dusting
crème fraîche, to serve

When there is no ripe fruit available, dried prunes are very good to use in a tart. If you soak them in hot Earl Grey tea, they will plump up and also absorb the flavour of any alcohol you may wish to add. In this recipe I've used Armagnac but you could replace it with a decent brandy. Makes a 26cm tart to serve 8.

prune and armagnac tart

1 Preheat the oven to 180°C. Line the tart case with baking parchment and fill with baking beans. Blind bake for 15 minutes until golden in colour. Remove the paper and baking beans, then return the tart case to the oven to bake for a further 5 minutes. Brush all over the inside of the case with egg wash to seal. Bake for another 5 minutes, then set aside. Leave the oven on.

2 Make the filling while the pastry case is baking. Put the teabag in a bowl and cover with boiling water. Add the prunes and leave to soak for 15 minutes. Drain the prunes (discard the tea bag and soaking water) and add the Armagnac to them. Leave to macerate for 20 minutes.

3 Meanwhile, whisk the eggs and caster sugar together with an electric mixer until pale, thick and doubled in volume. Add the vanilla seeds, clementine zest and juice, cream, almonds and flour and mix in gently but thoroughly.

4 Arrange the prunes evenly over the base of the tart case. Add any macerating liquid to the egg mixture, then carefully pour this over the prunes. Bake for about 20 minutes until the filling is golden brown and set. It should be springy and slightly puffy.

5 Cool to room temperature before dusting with sifted icing sugar and serving with crème fraîche.

1 x 26cm Sweet Pastry Case
   (see recipe on page 221)

For the filling
350g fresh walnut halves
50g dark soft brown sugar
20g plain flour
3 organic eggs
grated zest of 1 orange
   (preferably a blood orange)
juice of 3 oranges
   (preferably blood oranges)
seeds from ¼ vanilla pod
4 tbsp raw honey (chestnut
   honey is the nicest in this tart)
good-quality vanilla ice cream
   or crème fraîche, to serve

I love walnuts. If you are lucky enough to get fresh ones, this is a great dessert to use them in, although the tart can be made very successfully with dried walnuts. Serve this at room temperature – the honey, orange and walnuts need the cooling time to set together. Makes a 26cm tart to serve 8.

walnut, orange and honey tart

1 Preheat the oven to 180°C. Line the tart case with baking parchment and fill with baking beans. Blind bake for 15 minutes until golden in colour. Remove the paper and baking beans, then return the tart case to the oven to bake for a further 5 minutes. Set aside. Leave the oven on.

2 While the tart case is baking, toast the walnuts on a baking tray in the oven for 10 minutes. Remove any loose skins. Arrange the nuts in the tart case.

3 Combine the sugar and flour in a bowl. Whisk in the eggs followed by the orange zest and juice, vanilla seeds and honey. Pour this mixture over the walnuts.

4 Bake for 20–30 minutes until the filling is firm. Leave to cool before serving each slice with a scoop of vanilla ice cream.

super quick   quick   a little more time   **1½ hours,**
                                                                                       plus cooling
                                                                                       leisurely but worth it

400g 70% dark chocolate,
    broken up
6 organic eggs, separated
150g caster sugar
300ml double cream
50ml whisky
Crema di Mascarpone
    (see recipe on page 210),
    to serve

This cake has been on the restaurant menu from day one and is very popular. It is one of those cakes that looks like it may be heavy but is surprisingly light. As with all chocolate desserts, the better the chocolate you use, the better the cake will taste. Rich Crema di Mascarpone is delicious with the cake. Serves 8.

soft chocolate cake
with whisky

1 Preheat the oven to 150°C. Grease a 20cm round cake tin and line with baking parchment.

2 Melt the chocolate in a heatproof bowl set over a saucepan of hot water (the bottom of the bowl should not be in contact with the water). Remove from the heat and set aside to cool a bit.

3 Whisk the egg yolks with 100g sugar until pale in colour and increased in volume. In another bowl, whip 150ml cream with the whisky to soft peaks stage.

4 In another bowl, whisk the egg whites until frothy, then gradually whisk in the remaining sugar. Keep whisking until the whites are light and glossy and will make soft peaks when the whisk is lifted out.

5 Stir the melted chocolate and the remaining unwhipped cream into the yolk mixture. Fold in the whipped whisky cream, then gently fold in the whisked egg whites. Pour into the prepared tin.

6 Set the tin in a bain marie (a roasting tin filled with hot water: the water level should be right up to the rim of the cake tin). Bake for 45–60 minutes until the cake feels firm on the top but still has a slight wobble in the middle. Remove the tin from the bain marie and set on a wire rack. Leave to cool in the tin.

7 Serve the cake with some crema di mascarpone, if you like.

1.2 litres double cream
2 vanilla pods, split open lengthways
thinly peeled rind of 1 lemon
3 gelatine leaves
150ml cold milk
1 tbsp grappa
150g icing sugar, sifted

For the rhubarb
2 sticks rhubarb
150g vanilla sugar
thinly peeled rind and juice
  of 1 blood orange
5 tbsp Moscato d'Asti

Pannacotta – literally 'cooked cream' – has a lovely smooth texture, as long as you use the correct amount of gelatine. Too much will make it rubbery and not as appealing. Rhubarb has a very distinct flavour that complements the pannacotta. Cooking rhubarb with something sweet like Moscato wine makes its flavour better balanced and less sharp. Makes 8.

pannacotta
with rhubarb and vanilla

1 Heat 900ml cream with the vanilla pods and lemon rind until boiling, then simmer until reduced by a third. Pour into a large bowl set over ice and leave to cool.

2 Soak the gelatine leaves in the cold milk for 5–10 minutes until soft. Remove from the milk and reserve. Warm the milk gently until just below boiling point. Off the heat, add the soaked gelatine and stir until melted, then strain the milk into the reduced vanilla cream. Stir in the grappa. Leave to cool again, whisking every 5 minutes to prevent the mixture from going lumpy.

3 In a bowl, whip the remaining cream with the icing sugar to soft peaks. When the vanilla cream has cooled and reached the consistency of double cream, fish out the vanilla pods and lemon rind, then fold in the sweetened whipped cream.

4 Pour the mixture into cappuccino cups or other small moulds and leave to set in the fridge for at least 2 hours.

5 Meanwhile, prepare the rhubarb. Preheat the oven to 180°C. Cut the rhubarb into batons 5cm long and 2cm wide. Spread them in a baking dish and cover with the vanilla sugar. Add the orange rind and drizzle the orange juice and Moscato d'Asti over the rhubarb. Cover with foil and bake for 15 minutes until the rhubarb is tender but not stewed. Cool.

6 To serve, dip the cups in hot water for 5–10 seconds – the pannacotta should turn out easily (or you can serve in the cups). Use a small sharp knife to loosen the edges, if you need to. Top each pannacotta with some rhubarb and its juice.

200g caster sugar
400ml freshly squeezed
   blood orange juice

A very simple recipe, this is perfect as a refreshing sorbet after a meal or just to cool you down any time. If you can, use freshly squeezed blood oranges, although I have tried making the sorbet with Tropicana sanguinello blood orange juice and it did work well. Serves 4.

blood orange sorbet

1 Put the sugar in a saucepan with 100ml water and heat, stirring, until the sugar has dissolved. Leave to cool, then chill until cold.

2 Mix together the sugar syrup and orange juice. Pour into an ice cream machine and churn until softly set. Transfer to a freezerproof container and leave to 'ripen' in the freezer for 1 hour before serving. (The sorbet can be kept in the freezer for up to 2 months; before serving let it soften a bit for 5–10 minutes at room temperature.)

200g caster sugar
15 ripe white peaches
juice of 1 lemon

Peaches are so good on their own but puréeing them, adding a sugar syrup and freezing takes them to a new level. Luscious, ripe white peaches are the ones to use for this sorbet. It will be slightly pink, not white, because when you blanch the peaches the colour from their skins will penetrate into the flesh. Serves 6–8.

peach sorbet

1 Put the sugar in a saucepan with 100ml water and heat, stirring, until the sugar has dissolved. Leave this sugar syrup to cool completely.

2 Drop the peaches into a pan of boiling water and leave to blanch for 2 minutes. Drain and refresh in cold water. Peel the peaches (keep the skins).

3 Purée the peach flesh in a food processor, then pass through a sieve into a bowl. Put the peach skins in the sieve and press over the bowl to extract all their richly coloured juice. Add lemon juice and sugar syrup to taste – freezing will diminish the flavour so be sure the mixture is sweet.

4 Pour into an ice cream machine and churn until softly set. Transfer to a freezerproof container and leave to 'ripen' in the freezer for 1 hour before serving. (The sorbet can be kept in the freezer for up to 2 months; before serving let it soften a bit for 5–10 minutes at room temperature.)

For the pancakes
120g plain flour
2 medium eggs, beaten
300ml full-fat milk
25g unsalted butter, melted
a little extra virgin olive oil for the pan

For the chocolate and whisky sauce
100ml double cream
25ml whisky
100g 70% dark chocolate, chopped

To serve
1 tub good-quality vanilla ice cream
50g toasted flaked almonds

Pancakes, chocolate and vanilla ice cream – what could be better?! Serve the chocolate sauce warm so it melts the ice cream and makes a delicious mess. Serves 4.

pancakes
with ice cream and chocolate whisky sauce

1 Sift the flour into a mixing bowl. Make a well in the middle and add the eggs, milk and butter. Whisk these together, then bring in the flour from the sides so everything gets mixed together to make a smooth batter.

2 Heat a 20cm non-stick frying pan. Add a drop of olive oil and rub all over the pan with kitchen paper. Add a ladle of the pancake batter and quickly tilt the pan so the batter spreads over the surface evenly. Cook for 1 minute. Slip a palette knife under the pancake to be sure it is not sticking, then flip it over and cook the other side for 1 minute. Flip on to a plate. Repeat this process until you have made four good pancakes (the first one will probably not be perfect so you can feed it to the dog!).

3 To make the sauce, put the double cream and whisky into a small saucepan and bring to the boil for 1 second. Remove from the heat and add the chocolate. Let the chocolate soften and melt, then stir until smooth.

4 Lay a pancake on each serving plate. Put a scoop of vanilla ice cream in the middle of each pancake, then fold over. Spoon on the chocolate sauce and finish with a sprinkle of toasted flaked almonds.

3 punnets fresh raspberries
Almond Croquante (see page 219)

For the crema di mascarpone
200g mascarpone
seeds from ½ vanilla pod
50g icing sugar, sifted
2 tbsp Marsala or to taste
150ml double cream

I love this recipe because it is so easy.
It is perfect to put in the middle of the
table for a group of people to share
(or fight over). The slightly sharp flavour
of fresh raspberries is perfect with the
sweet mascarpone cream and caramel.
Make the Almond Croquante ahead to
keep this dessert super quick to make.
Serves 4.

english raspberries
with crema di mascarpone
and almond croquante

1 To make the crema di mascarpone,
beat the mascarpone with the vanilla
seeds and icing sugar. Beat in the
Marsala. In a separate bowl, whip the
cream to soft peaks. Fold the cream
into the mascarpone mixture.

2 Spoon the crema di mascarpone
on to a serving dish. Scatter over
the raspberries and sprinkle with
almond croquante.

200g dried whole apricots
    (without stones)
1 tbsp icing sugar
50ml Amaretto liqueur
1–2 tubs good-quality vanilla
    ice cream to serve
50g toasted flaked almonds,
    to serve

Dried apricots soaked in Amaretto liqueur
are absolutely delicious. Some good quality
vanilla ice cream is perfect with them.
Serves 4.

macerated apricots
with amaretto and toasted almonds

1 Put the dried apricots in a bowl and pour
over boiling water to cover. Leave to soak
for 5 minutes (or longer if the apricots are
very dry), then drain off the water.

2 Break the apricots into halves and place,
hollow side up, in a shallow dish. Sprinkle
over the icing sugar and then the Amaretto.
Leave to macerate for 5 minutes.

3 Spoon the apricots over scoops of vanilla
ice cream. Drizzle over the apricot juices
and scatter the toasted almonds on top.
Serve immediately.

4 tbsp raisins
2 tbsp Alnwick rum,
    plus extra for serving
350ml double cream
100g caster sugar
4 organic egg yolks

These are simple but taste delicious, a perfect dinner party dessert with very little effort. I like to use Alnwick rum, which is very dark, almost black, with a distinctive flavour, but you can use any dark rum. Serve the pots straight from the fridge. Serves 4.

rum and raisin cream pots

1 Preheat the oven to 170°C. Soak the raisins in hot water for 5 minutes, then drain and mix with the rum. Set aside.

2 Heat the cream and sugar in a saucepan until the sugar dissolves and the mixture reaches about 90°C on a cooking thermometer.

3 Meanwhile, whisk the egg yolks in a bowl, just to mix. Add the hot cream mixture, stirring constantly. Strain through a fine sieve into a jug. Add the raisins in rum.

4 Pour into four ramekins. Set them in a small deep oven tray and add enough hot water to the tray to come two-thirds of the way up the sides of the ramekins. Cover the tray with foil and bake for 15 minutes.

5 Lift the ramekins out of the water and leave to cool down, then chill. Serve with an extra dash of rum on top.

**40-45 minutes,
plus cooling**
a little more time

400g blanched (skinned) almonds
4 organic eggs, separated
250g caster sugar
150g plain flour
250g unsalted butter
250g 70% dark chocolate

These cookies are based on a Torta Caprese, which is the best chocolate and almond cake you will ever taste. Of course, anything with dark chocolate and almonds is going to taste good! Makes about 12.

chocolate and almond cookies

1 Preheat the oven to 180°C. Spread the almonds on a baking sheet and lightly toast in the oven as it heats up. Line 1–2 baking sheets with baking parchment.

2 Beat the egg yolks with the sugar in a large bowl until pale, light and creamy. Add the flour and mix well. Set aside.

3 Gently heat the butter in a small pan until it has just melted; remove from the heat. Finely chop the toasted almonds and roughly chop the chocolate.

4 In another large bowl, whisk the egg whites until soft peaks form when the whisk is lifted from the bowl.

5 Fold the almonds and chocolate into the yolk mixture followed by the melted butter and then the whisked egg whites, folding just until combined.

6 Place spoonfuls of the mixture, well spaced apart, on the lined baking sheets. Bake for 12–15 minutes until the cookies are set and crisp on the outside (they should still be soft in the middle). Transfer to wire racks to cool before serving.

For the sweet pastry
150g plain flour, plus extra for dusting
50g icing sugar, sifted
100g unsalted butter, chilled
1 organic egg yolk

For the topping
80g sultanas
3 tbsp sweet Marsala wine
450g sheep's ricotta
100g caster sugar
1 tbsp plain flour
3 organic eggs, separated
4 tbsp double cream
4 tbsp crème fraîche
seeds from 1 vanilla pod
¼ tsp sea salt

This is probably my favourite dessert – a rich and creamy cheesecake on a sweet pastry base. By using ricotta rather than cream cheese, the filling is lighter, with Marsala adding its wonderful flavour. It's perfect for entertaining because you can make it the day before. Try the cheesecake with macerated pears, which have such a lovely texture and flavour. Serves 8.

ricotta cheesecake

1 First make the pastry. Put the flour, icing sugar and butter in a food processor and pulse until the mixture resembles fine breadcrumbs. Add the egg yolk and pulse for 10 seconds, then tip into a bowl and mix briefly by hand into a dough. Cover the bowl and leave the pastry to rest in the fridge for 1 hour.

2 Line a 23cm springform tin with baking parchment. Roll out the pastry on a lightly floured surface and use to line the base of the tin. Leave to rest in the fridge for 30 minutes.

3 Preheat the oven to 180°C. Bake the pastry base for 20 minutes until set and golden brown. Set aside to cool. Turn the oven down to 160°C.

4 Make the topping while the pastry is cooling. First put the sultanas in a bowl with the Marsala wine to soak. Meanwhile, combine the ricotta, sugar and flour in a large bowl and beat until smooth. Add the egg yolks, double cream, crème fraîche and vanilla seeds, then stir in the sultanas and Marsala wine.

5 In another bowl, whisk the egg whites with the salt until stiff peaks form. Fold into the ricotta mixture. Pour into the springform tin over the baked base. Bake for 50 minutes or until the filling is just set in the middle. Allow to cool, then chill before serving.

basic recipes

almond croquante

200g whole blanched (skinned) almonds
200g caster sugar

This is delicious sprinkled over sweet fresh berries topped with cream or ice cream, or a mascarpone cream (see the recipe for English Raspberries with Crema di Mascarpone on page 210). Makes about 400g.

1 Preheat the oven to 180°C. Spread the almonds on a small baking tray and roast for 5 minutes until they are a light golden colour. Leave to one side.

2 Put the sugar in a saucepan and add 1 tablespoon water. Cook, without stirring, on a medium heat until the sugar melts and turns a light golden colour. Add the almonds and carry on cooking for 1 minute. Pour on to an oiled baking sheet and leave to cool and set.

3 Roughly break up the croquante and put into a food bag. Bash with a rolling pin to break up into pieces of whatever size and shape you like. The croquante can be kept in an airtight container for up to a month.

chicken stock

1 chicken carcass
2 celery sticks, roughly chopped
2 carrots, roughly chopped
1 leek, roughly chopped
a handful of parsley stalks
1 bay leaf

You will always find a plastic mineral water bottle full of chicken stock in my fridge. Makes about 1 litre.

1 Put the carcass in a large pot with about 2 litres water and bring to the boil. Skim off all the scum that rises, then add the vegetables and herbs. Reduce the heat and simmer for 1 hour.

2 Strain through a sieve and cool. The stock can be kept in an airtight container in the fridge for up to 3 days, or frozen. It will probably set to a jelly and a layer of fat will form on the surface (skim most of this off before using the stock).

salsa d'erbe

100g flat-leaf parsley leaves
50g wild rocket
30g mint leaves
25g picked marjoram leaves
50g basil leaves
2 anchovy fillets (packed in oil),
    drained and chopped into a paste
50g small capers in vinegar,
    drained and finely chopped
½ garlic clove, peeled
75g ciabatta crumbs (without crusts),
    soaked in water to moisten, then
    squeezed out
1 tsp Dijon mustard
1 tsp red wine vinegar
50ml extra virgin olive oil
sea salt and freshly ground black pepper

This is delicious spread on crostini and topped with a slice of fresh ricotta. It also makes a great accompaniment for a meat dish such as Pork Loin Wrapped in Coppa di Parma (see recipe on page 165). Serves 4–6.

1 Using a sharp knife, finely chop all the herbs with the anchovies, capers, garlic and bread (the moist bread helps to bind the ingredients together). Transfer to a bowl.

2 Add the mustard and vinegar and season with salt and pepper, then stir in the olive oil. This is best used freshly made, but any leftovers can be kept in a covered bowl or jar in the fridge for a couple of days – put a layer of olive oil on the surface of the salsa to prevent it from discolouring.

salsa verde

100g flat-leaf parsley leaves
50g wild rocket
30g mint leaves
25g picked marjoram leaves
4 tbsp extra virgin olive oil
2 anchovy fillets (packed in oil), drained
1½ tbsp capers in vinegar, drained
¼ garlic clove, peeled
1 tbsp Dijon mustard, or to taste
sea salt and freshly ground black pepper

Literally 'green sauce', this has many variations, using different herbs and flavourings. It is a really useful sauce to serve with all kinds of meat, fish, poultry and vegetable dishes. Serves 4–6.

1 Chop the herbs really finely and transfer to a bowl. Immediately cover with the olive oil so the herbs don't turn brown.

2 Pound the anchovies, capers and garlic together using a pestle and mortar to make a paste.

3 Mix in the herbs (with the oil) and add Dijon mustard to taste. Season with salt and pepper (be careful with the salt as anchovies and capers are both quite salty). This is best used freshly made, but any leftovers can be kept in a covered bowl or jar in the fridge for a couple of days – put a layer of olive oil on the surface of the salsa to prevent it from discolouring.

pesto

½ garlic clove, peeled
handful of basil leaves
2 tbsp pine nuts, preferably Mediterranean
2 tbsp freshly grated Parmesan cheese
240ml extra virgin olive oil, plus extra for sealing
sea salt and freshly ground black pepper

This classic sauce has so many uses – it can be stirred into soups (see Minestrone Primavera on page 55), tossed with freshly cooked pasta or vegetables, or dolloped on top of bruschetta. Pesto is best when freshly made, but it can be kept in the fridge for up to a week – spoon the pesto into a jar or bowl and add a layer of olive oil on the surface (this will prevent the pesto from oxidising and turning brown), then cover tightly. Serves 4.

1 Crush the garlic with a pinch of salt using a mortar and pestle, or on a chopping board using a spoon – the garlic should form a soft paste.

2 Transfer the garlic to a food processor and add the basil, pine nuts, Parmesan and 2 tablespoons water. Blitz until all the ingredients are finely chopped and a smooth paste has formed.

3 Add the olive oil and pulse for 2 seconds (if you pulse longer the oil will emulsify). Check and adjust the seasoning.

fish stock

400g bones and heads from white fish
   such as sole or plaice
2 carrots, cut into 2cm pieces
1 leek, cut into 2cm pieces
2 celery sticks, cut into 2cm pieces
5 parsley stalks
sprig of thyme
1 tsp sea salt

I think fish stock should be cooked longer than most recipes call for, because you want to get as much flavour from the bones as possible. Fish stock doesn't need to be crystal clear. You can season at the end, but by putting the salt in at the beginning of cooking the stock will have a more developed flavour. Makes about 1 litre.

1 Remove the eyes and gills from the fish heads, and give the heads and bones a good rinse.

2 Put the fish heads and bones into a pan with 1.5 litres cold water. Bring up to a simmer, then skim off all the foam that has come to the surface.

3 Add the vegetables, herbs and salt. Simmer gently for 30–40 minutes so the stock has lots of flavour. Strain and cool down. The stock can be kept in an airtight container in the fridge for 2–3 days, or frozen.

mayonnaise

1 egg yolk
½ tsp Dijon mustard
juice of ½ lemon
250ml mild olive oil
1 tbsp warm water
sea salt and freshly ground black pepper

I use a china bowl when making mayonnaise and aïoli because if you use a metal bowl and metal whisk, the friction from beating two metals together will give the mayonnaise a metallic taste. Makes about 300ml.

1 Put the egg yolk, mustard, lemon juice and ½ teaspoon salt in a china or earthenware bowl. Whisk to break up and mix the ingredients, then begin adding the olive oil very slowly, whisking steadily.

2 When the mayonnaise starts to look thick and will not take any more oil, whisk in the warm water. Then continue to add the olive oil, whisking constantly. Check the seasoning at the end, adding more salt if needed and some pepper.

aïoli

1 garlic clove, peeled
2 egg yolks
juice of ½ lemon
300ml mild olive oil
1 tbsp warm water
sea salt and freshly ground black pepper

This garlicky mayonnaise should be really thick, which is why there is more oil than in a basic mayonnaise recipe. Makes about 350ml.

1 Crush the garlic with 1 teaspoon salt until it becomes a paste. This is best done using a pestle and mortar or on a chopping board using a spoon.

2 Put the egg yolks in a china or earthenware bowl and add the crushed garlic and lemon juice. Mix together, then start slowly adding the olive oil, whisking constantly. When the aïoli begins to look very thick, add the warm water, then continue whisking in the remaining olive oil.

3 Check the seasoning at the end, adding more salt if needed and some pepper.

sweet pastry case

250g plain flour, plus extra for dusting
75g icing sugar, sifted
180g unsalted butter, chilled
2 organic egg yolks

Makes a 26cm tart case.

1 Put the flour, icing sugar and butter in a food processor and pulse until the mixture resembles fine breadcrumbs. Add the egg yolks and pulse for 10 seconds, then tip into a bowl and mix briefly by hand into a dough.

2 Cover the bowl and leave the pastry to rest in the fridge for 1 hour.

3 Roll out the pastry on a lightly floured surface and press into a 26cm fluted, loose-bottomed tart tin to line evenly. Leave to rest in the fridge for 30 minutes before baking as directed in the recipe.

index